WISDOM
of the
DRUIDS

- The Book of Nabelkos -

Sᴀᴍᴏɴɪᴏꜱ 3781 **M.T.**
Aɴ**IEM**

Given by
Gwenaël d'Echebrune
Translated from Breton by Drustanos
Received by Bruno Piaud
Translated in English by Jean-Marie Avril

Library of the Green Flame
Theurgia Publications
www.theurgia.us

Publishers: Jean-Louis de Biasi - Patricia Bourin

Theurgia Publications © 2020
304 A. Jones Blvd #3664, Las Vegas, NV, 89107, USA
secretary@theurgia.us
Made in the United- tates of America
ISBN: 978-1-926451-30-5

Discover other publications of "Theurgia"
www.theurgia.us

Acknowledgements

I want first to recognize and salute Mr. Bruno Piaud who channeled this powerful text now part of the Druidic heritage. We must be humble when an authentic voice coming from an initiate gives us a gift such as the Nabelkos.

I want also to give a deep gratitude to Jean-Marie Avril who did the hard work of translating the book and authorizing this publication. For those who do not know, translating a traditional text is very complicated and exhausting. Thanks to him many generations will be able to learn and meditate this revelation.

CONTENTS

FOREWORD

The Western spiritual tradition has a long history dating back to the dawn of humanity. One of the consequences of Christianity was to hide and distort the thousands of years that preceded it. Whether around the Mediterranean basin or in the lands of Europe, rites handed down from generation to generation formed the real basis of this Western tradition. To believe that they were replaced for the better by a new religion is a mistake. The notion of progress does not exist for religious or spiritual systems. Gods and Goddesses are rejected, beaten, and sometimes replaced by new ones. Some disappear for a while and reappear in cycles that initiates have learned to decipher.

At the dawn of time, what is today called shamanism was one of the most original forms of religion. We can still see its vestiges on the walls of the oldest painted caves and in the deepest parts of our psyche. These practices did not disappear. They adapted and developed. The Nordic, Celtic, Gallic, then Gallo-Roman religions are expressions of this original spiritual heritage. The various cults then practiced, such as those of deities of springs, mountains, rivers, or caves demonstrate this continuity. It was the case up to the 5th century AD and continued hidden until today. The Breton pardons, the pilgrimage of the 7 holy founders, the Calvaries at the crossroads are all traces diverted from the original pagan tradition. This foreword is not intended to develop the historical aspect of paganism and Druidism in Gaul. Nor is the goal to compare these theologies and their consequences on the conscience of peoples. It is important to remember; however, that from the point of view of the Western spiritual tradition, 1,500 years of development of a new religion is a very short period. It is also fundamental to realize, as I stressed before, that new religions do not erase old traditions. It is the same with Goddesses and Gods.

Shamanic, Nordic, Celtic and Druidic traditions are not reawakened, because they never ceased to be. They simply remain hidden behind the curtain of mist that veils the true access to Avalon and the land of the ancestors. A pure heart can always ask for access to this place. The Gods will then send the signs that each initiate would recognize.

I remember very well my first steps in this Druidic tradition. As I was walking to a clearing to receive a Kuldean Druidic transmission, a mighty raptor appeared in the sky holding a long serpent in its claws. He was flying in the same direction as me; as the snake still fidgeted in its talons. The power of this symbol, announcing the passage which was about to unfold, was very significant for me. During the 80's I pursued this shamanic and Druidic path in France. The veils were lifted one by one as meetings in places of power transmitted to me the consecrations of these traditions. I had the privilege of practicing these rituals in some little-known, if not secret, places in different regions of France. This was before the New Age wave turned the traditions of this country into a romantic and sanitized fiction. I have been able to invoke ancestral powers in ancient caves in the Basque country where stalactites were still surrounded by ribbons of fabric and flowers. I have greeted the fairies and elves in the morning dew near unknown Breton springs. Dressed in white and wearing the golden Tribann on my forehead, I invoked the ancestors under respectable dolmens and menhirs. Wearing the same ritual clothes, I harvested the mistletoe, in the traditional way, while my daughters, also dressed in white, held the white sheet.

I have been able to cross the veils of mist several times and listen to the voices of the elders.

Later, becoming Grand Master of Aurum Solis[1], I received another lineage, and the titles of Grand Druid and High Priest of the Celtic Mysteries.

Two of my Aurum Solis predecessors had important responsibilities in the founding and development of two British Druidic Orders: The "Druid Order" and the "Order of Bards, Ovates and Druids."

Because of what I received, Aurum Solis today preserves several authentic Druid lineages united in the "Order of the Green Flame." This is not an independent Druidic Order. On the contrary, this structure is an integral part of the Aurum Solis, and is offered to initiates who wish to deepen this important aspect of the tradition. The pre-Christian, Gallo-Roman, Celtic, or Druidic festivals are celebrated and generally

---

[1] www.aurumsolis.org

preceded by the Rota Fulgens Solis ritual. Some of these rites can be performed within the family, while others involve only initiates. Gradual shamanic initiations are sometimes offered to certain companions who have been chosen for their honesty, humility, and psychological stability. As for the present book of Nabelkos, it has been for many years entrusted to the study of adepts. This desire to remain a private structure reserved for a few, makes it possible to avoid any form of religious drift.

Among the fascinating traditions coming from Gaul, today's France, Druidism and the Celtic mysteries have acquired an essential place that has too often been neglected by the occultists of the 19th century. As I have just recalled, some individuals have had the privilege of opening the mists and receiving messages from the immortal deities. Characteristic of a land and lineage, these communications are important. The "Book of Nabelkos," which has been translated into English by Jean-Marie Avril belongs to this story. You can find more information about the background of this revelation and the book's doctrine in the afterword to this edition. It was channeled by Gwenael d'Echebrune. Bruno Piaud also played an important role in the history of the "Book of Nabelkos" and deserves to be saluted. This book constituted the doctrinal and prophetic heart of an Order bearing the beautiful name of "Hermetic Order of the Silver Ermine" (French: Ordre Hermétique de l'Hermine d'Argent). The latter was created by the Breton Pierre de Mauclerc in the 1960s and continued to exist for a few years.

It is a magnificent example that demonstrates the vitality of a pre-Christian tradition still alive today. Its style manifests its roots and the authenticity of the shamanic experience that gave birth to it. This is how the true initiates of this tradition, whether bards or druids, reveal certain messages at certain points in history. It is the same for this present edition.

I wish you a fruitful and respectful meditation of these sacred words crossing the mists of time, testimony of a tradition still alive!

Jean-Louis de Biasi

Las Vegas, August 2020.

I. THE GREAT REVELATION

Say:

1 - May Lug be glorified forever! Praise to the Master of the Worlds, the First, the Strong, He who leads us to the right way, The Very Wise, the Handsome, the King above all the High Kings of light. May his cause be exalted above All!

2 - The Giver of all possibilities, the Treasurers of all treasures, he gives only through the medium of His agents.

3 - the Sovereign who is the Lord of the Initiates, the Eternal Guide of seekers, the many-sided Artist, He gives through the intervention/medium of Dana, through the intervention/medium of the three Gods of Dana, through the intervention/medium of the Harp Player, through the intervention/medium of the Chronicler, through the intervention/medium of the Combatant, through the intervention/medium of the Healer, through the intervention/medium of the Cup-Bearer, through the intervention/medium of the Bronze-Smith [bronze craftsman], through the intervention/medium of the Carpenter, through the intervention/medium of the Blacksmith.

4 - Today, the Cup-Bearer pours in a flood-like manner the divine foods for the Galaadians, freedom to His servants, beauty to His worshippers, harmony to those who act, the Champions of His cause.

5 - Today, let's pay attention to the Voice of He who bless the Tree; let's stand up and follow He who took us away from darkness, the Help during peril, the Liberator.

6 - Today, happy is he who, from His seals, recognizes the 666 Star as a sign of rallying.

7 - Today, today with the sword of his teaching, with enthusiasm in our hearts, the fervour of our souls, the might of our energies, we sow our land under the Sun.

II. THE CALL

1

1- He says: I call from the kingdom of eternity all the clans of the Earth, and I invite them to take their share of the fruits of the Tree of faithfulness.

2 - He says: Listen to my Call and join [again], for the first among you is awaiting the last among you.

3 - He says: It has been a long time that you are enslaved: why don't you stand up? Leave the aggressive troop, turn your eyes towards the new Dawn, I created it so that it shines on you.

4 - He says: I have in advance assigned to each his share, leaving to you the care to make it bear fruit.

5 - He says: Happy is he who, perceiving the Call, is touched by conviction; that one takes the path of light.

6 - He says: Truly, I fix a new 'today' for those who aspire to Total freedom.

7 - He says: Understand, short is the human life on the Earth formed from the ashes of the dead; one must not lose an instant of the passing time.

2

1 - He says: Do not seek what perishes, direct yourself towards what is better, towards the prettiest fruits of the Tree of Life.

2 - He says: Happy is he who remains young all his life, the adolescent full of great hopes, free like the morning breeze, I will allow for free to drink [of] the source of the water of life.

3 - He says: I am not happy with anyone who doesn't rise, and doesn't seek to go beyond their limits.

4 - He says: As to the draft dodgers, the torment to come will have no comparison; many will be drowned in their blood with the steel they feed on.

5 - He says: Roots must be strongly set within the entrails, the bowels and the hearts so that the branches rise up to the sky and beyond.

6 - He says: Truly, the sound of the golden bell of the Call rings in the heart of the livings like a smooth enchantment, but those who don't hear it live in vain.

7 - He says: Understand, when you have faith in God, you attract to yourself the mark of God's Power.

3

1 - He says: Everything that diminishes slavery and increases freedom is worthy the attention, but one deserves freedom and life only when one must win them every day.

2 - He says: If, fearing the fruit, you dry [out] the tree trunk, you will get illness, sorrows and death.

3 - He says: He whom you bear carry within you will easily climb Hierarchy's steps.

4 - He says: Life is not a vain detour towards death; each defeat, each victory uniquely contributes to elevate you.

5 - He says: Get rid of your bonds and become a beautiful light at the top of the Tree of marvelous glory.

6 - He says: Truly, things will not be the way you want them to be, Things will be as I decide them to be, no more no less.

7 - He says: Is vanquished only he who did not want to be victor.

4

1 - He says: I call you to the sojourn of bliss, Come to seek refuge in there.

2 - He says: Like a lion who breaks the bars of its cage, break your bonds and be free forever.

3 - He says: Seek to know yourself, you will discover within you countless spiritual treasures, you will become a torch for those who walk in darkness and a rallying point for those who are scattered.

4 - He says: Avoid anything that can make you fall, anything that can humiliate you and anything that impoverish you; seek everything that make you progress, anything that can enrich you for you have a right to wealth and glory.

5 - He says: Everything that is inferior to you is a barrier, and each inch of land must be won against considerable resistance; cultivate patience and perseverance. Each day is followed by its morrow; do not despair of victory when fate imposes on you a dire situation.

6 - He says: Truly, light is he who knows the pure Self [or 'I'] and freedom, he can walk on thorns and swords without any risk.

7 - He says: Understand, You must not seek refuge in centuries past. From the depths of your being, bring about the spring

of a new world and you will shine like a star in the night..

5

1 - He says: I call upon the champions who attach suns to the wheel of their chariots pulled by untameable, winged and white-mane steeds.

2 - He says: The time has come for you to serve my Cause, for the time is not far when all the Earth clan will gather in my Empire.

3 - He says: Live each minute as if it was the last, and think that the occasion/opportunity showing itself may never come again.

4 - He says: God announces himself through the mouth of people doing His will, and who having reached the shore leave you with the raft to cross the furious current/flow.

5 - He says: If you can and know to acknowledge him as the Unique, then you will know everything; if you cannot and don't know to acknowledge him as the Unique, all your science will only be ignorance.

6 - He says: Truly the source of error resides in denying him, putting one's trust in others instead of Him and refusing to conform to what He has ordained.

7 - He says: Understand, liberation may demand an extremely long time, but whether the day of reckoning is soon or distant, it will inevitably come.

6

1 - He says: I do not seek to make a profit; I work so that you join me and there is no one lost.

2 - He says: Stop behaving like machines, Tackle the real and true sense of your activities; so that each starts bearing fruits and a world of life will take place.

3 - He says: when a desire animates a man, it is up to him to achieve it, for you can know the existence of the Creator only by fulfilling His wish.

4 - He says: Do not deprive yourself of what has been created for you; direct yourself to what causes good fortune, happiness and joy.

5 - He says: Sad will be the fate of he or she whose words exceed their deeds.

6 - He says: Truly, Eternity can be chosen only by the one concerned by it in the first place.

7 - He says: Understand, while one seeks the vision of another one instead of Him, and while one seeks this vision in some place other than in one's very soul, one raves and drift in impossibility and uncertainty.

7

1 - He says: You must accomplish, in a diligent fashion, with the most perfect elation and the liveliest ardor, everything that the Lord of Light commands you to do.

2 - He says: Work to conquer the power of living; meditate on the glory of He who created the universe; may He enlighten your mind!

3 - He says: The thing that can be/is the most elevated on earth is an infinite distance of/from what the divine is and of/from what you will become.

4 - He says: Compared with your evil deeds, what have you to put on the scales? You are not happy as you are prisoner of your vain actions. It is only from a total freedom that you will be able to forge your divine nature.

5 - He says: Listen to the Call of the Lord endowed with the Inexpressible Might, the Guide outside the path leading astray; put His mark on your right hand and leave behind the darkness that surround you.

6 - He says: Truly, Where the beginning is, there also resides the end.

7 - He says: Understand, I know what you wish for and I am with you everywhere.

8

1 - He says: All your past was the unfolding of a betrayal, and the darkness was forged by your refusal to acknowledge Me.

2 - He says: From the moment when you will understand that you exactly live in the world you deserve; you will recognize in somebody else's errors your own errors.

3 - He says: I establish war among the princes who carry bloody shields; I will choose men slain by the weapons they have forged for themselves.

4 - He says: He who has been liberated rises up to the level of the high branches of the Tree; He who refuses and stands up will be thrown down(wards).

5 - He says: Until when won't you find your ancient rank? In the mixed region, each hunter has a certain game, I will have for you arrows in My quiver.

6 - He says: Truly, each one of you is recognized according to the shining of his own light.

7 - He says: Understand, when doubts are severed, contrary deeds perish.

9

1 - He says: He who was named King over the High Kings, Master of the Gwenved, the kingdom of shining beauty, His Power inhabits all beings here-below. He is the Lord of all things, may you never forget it and may you never forget Him.

2 - He says: I made sure that the lights above the Horizon shine so that they help you reach your highest aim. Open your eyes upon what is hidden, stand up and seek without respite what leads to fulfilment.

3 - He says: A brave soldier for God's Cause doesn't attach his heart to transient values.

4 - He says: Forget the day that has been removed from your existence, and you will attain without difficulty your heart's desires.

5 - He says: Everything occurs to be used, all exists in order to be transformed.

6 - He says: Truly, He who ignores Me cannot for long resound the strings of his harp.

7 - He says: Understand, Those who are in obvious error do not respond to the Call, I will make sure that their works are vain and they will return to the dwelling of ice.

10

1 - He says: No one can run away from death in this universe; Make sure you do not die in a state of heedlessness, in the manner of a decaying carcass.

2 - He says: You cannot think of the divine in emphasising one half of your being and dismissing the other half.

3 - He says: Do not seek anything for yourself, except what can provide you with is necessary to assist you in the task you have to do.

4 - He says: All must be converted into means to bring experience into the perfection of the constant and permanent state.

5 - He says: Deeds without belief are not fertile and useless.

6 - He says: Truly, He is the Pourer, the Master of drops and waves; without Him, there would be neither rain nor wind, neither fine weather nor harvest. Those who prefer Him instead of any other face enter into freedom.

7 - He says: Understand, I call you to be free men instead of slaves; there is no stable refuge as long as your life is not strengthened.

11

1 - He says: Follow the Witness of the period, the Teacher of the cycle.

2 - He says: I practice no discrimination among the bearers of My message, for they all have a single and identical aim, and the riddle of the one is the secret of the other.

3 - He says: There is a fine princely destiny for he who turns his heart towards the Generous One.

4 - He says: Get started to know His desire, He will provide you with the most advantageous lot.

5 - He says: It is to escape from darkness that the seed works hard to germinate and the bud tries hard to open out, but can an empty pod sprout?

6 - He says: Truly, fervour, confidence and detachment are necessary for the growth in the secrecy of this freedom that will restore you in the Life everlasting.

7 - He says: Understand, you have to destroy the old structures and build a new kingdom both mighty and splendid.

12

1 - He says: The Liberator is within yourself; make sure He is the focus of all your being.

2 - He says: Where does this despondency come from at the time of peril? You have invented sadness, suffering and all the pangs of sickness, that is why the secrets you have believed to discover are only mirages on your astray-leading tracks.

3 - He says: Your discover beauty and deity within each thing if you possess eyes worthy to see both.

4 - He says: Becomes the fruit of all the desires dawning within you.

5 - He says: Priceless and beyond reckoning are the jewels hidden in the body's temple, But scarce are those who discover them.

6 - He says: Truly, the Call rings alongside the cycles in the whole of Creation.

7 - He says: Understand, It matters that you join you major exhalations in order to speed up the transformation of all things and thus allow all and each to re-enter the Highest State.

13

1 - He says: He who elevates by degrees will trace on you, with His Fire hand, the attestation of your intuition.

2 - He says: The sacred is what brings freedom: the profanes is what chains up. Break your deadly bonds in order to enable the spark to return towards the inferno from which it comes from.

3 - He says: He who heals himself cannot find a better doctor: seek a remedy to your ill otherwise you will attain pain without a remedy.

4 - He says: Drop what is secondary to concentrate on the main thing; deposit your burdens in the hands of He who can carry all, otherwise your labour will be only an infinite toil in a limitless desert.

5 - He says: the Universe is only a springboard, a ladder climbing up to the imperishable marvels; each victory over yourself allows you to go a step of the ladder further up.

6 - He says: Truly, I call you but never impose Myself on you.

7 - He says: Understand, unless you reach the last step of the ladder, you will never enter again the Eternal Dwelling.

14

1 - He says: Reign, Power, Might and Glory belong to The Lord of the Eternal Summer. May His will be done within and among you.

2 - He says: Doing what He asks you to do is not obeying a diktat but responding to a personal need.

3 - He says: Falsity is many but Truth is one and will surely triumph.

4 - He says: You possess all the power that you want; But the cauldron of the Master of the Abyss, gently warmed by the breath of nine virgins, doesn't boil the food of the cowards; Pearls circles are on the top of it.

5 - He says: Everything is possible with God. Those who have withdrawn from the Light, if they say yes to the Call and commune with His Will, will find their way towards Realisation.

6 - He says: Truly, the refusal to fulfil his destiny identifies man with circumstances and contexts.

7 - He says: Understand, great terror comes from false security and bogus safety.

15

1 - He says: I have created the Tree for the welfare of the questers, and as they rise further up from branch to branch, I make them aware of the aim of their movement and development.

2 - He says: All the planes of Creation and the all the Gods are included in man's body.

3 - He says: When you walk, remain composed and remain cool, many will stand up following your example.

4 - He says: Light's fruits bear all the marks of beauty.

5 - He says: Do not despise even the insect, for it too possesses ardor in its heart, and on its path and in its own way it will fulfil itself like and no less than a lion.

6 - He says: Truly, nothing is demanded beyond the tariff.

7 - He says: Understand, there is in a single star enough to melt all the ice of Yenved.

16

1 - He says: Cursed be those who remain deaf to the Call and totally blind by the crassest ignorance; cursed be those who wallow in the mire with the disgusting Fomoire.

2 - He says: The fire rises and the stone falls: take advantage of all favorable opportunities, lighten up and rejoice.

3 - He says: Nor more than one is able to catch air with a hook, so neither can the man, Whether with inspiration, sincere faith or with the sense of what he's actually saying, force his way through to the heart of another.

4 - He says: All beings are connected to/with their own nature, and it's within it that they must seek perfection.

5 - He says: In this world, you can reach the Eternal only through the transient, the real through the unreal.

6 - He says: Truly, all of what is given is only supply for the road, but you still continue to ignore the value of the life that I grant you.

7 - He says: Understand, intelligent people chose carefully, but foolish people chose foolishly.

17

1 - He says: Suffering and torments are bad dreams from which one must wake up; then your efforts will recognized/acknowledged and there will be a reward.

2 - He says: whether you are master of a huge amount or a small amount, everything becomes beneficial to whom directs his or her soul only towards Him.

3 - He says: All must die three times before tasting of the Supreme Great Bliss.

4 - He says: Leaving everything is winning everything; leaving everything is leaving the illusion to follow Him who is everything.

5 - He says: Establish yourself in the Cause of the Lord of Light as strongly and immutably as a mountain.

6 - He says: Truly, birth and death are only (processes of) change.

7 - He says: Understand, Your life will not end before its due time, that is why when death occurs, it is unwise to try running away from the inevitable destiny.

18

1 - He says: All of you are the fruits of the same Tree, the leaves of the same branch. You have been created to enjoy the same rights and take part in the same advantages, but since the Great Separation, you have been busy in killing your nature.

2 - He says: Do your prayers and flatteries really matter to Me? Wake up and I will enlighten you.

3 - He says: What freezes in Yenved is the 'no'.

4 - He says: There are signs put in order and they are like warnings.

5 - He says: You must always will/wish for more. Surpass yourself, and while at this task, do perish on the path leading to the Supreme Inn.

6 - He says: Truly, he who betrays God betrays his brother, nothing can divert him from evil.

7 - He says: Understand, whomever claims for himself only what I want for all to enjoy, and wants to take for himself as his good what belong to all, that one will be thrown down in the frozen hell.

19

1 - He says: The Provider of all goods must sought for his own sake and not for His gifts.

2 - He says: The incomplete ones do not possess the complete richness, they leave this world with regret and without having understood the goal of coming, stopping and departing.

3 - He says: The Divine doesn't reveal itself to a seeker satisfied with lesser results.

4 - He says: No work, which achievement costs nothing, attracts My Blessing on itself.

5 - He says: The Lord of Light is the most beautiful of all forms, and Beauty is His Holy Action.

6 - He says: Truly, Who else, but Him, is your ecstasy of living?

7 - He says: Understand, He who has rescued you from the land of perdition, His Hand knows the measure, It will give in to your desires that are too impatient, but It will be close to whomever surrenders to it.

20

1 - He says: The Creator has a plan to defeat the Abyss; He has sown islands crowned with green-ness and abundant with game.

His Might is Great, His Work is Beautiful and His Generosity is Supreme.

2 - He says: Everything that increase and everything that diminishes must be picked up at each moment in both a continual welcome and a continual detachment.

3 - He says: I do not spare you tribulations; you must acquire the strength to prevail over obstacles.

4 - He says: Things that must happen to you (are) hasten(ing); what you didn't foresee will realised at the end.

5 - He says: Men without light who carry within the curse of their existence encounter misfortunes.

6 - He says: Truly, dying is the best deal if it occurs in time.

7 - He says: Understand, whomever is protected by God has nothing to fear from neither fire nor water.

21

1 - He says: Do submit yourself. Submitting one's self means dedicating to Him all that you have in you, to Offer him all that you are and all that you have.

2 - He says: Each receives what properly owned to him, but God takes the thing you fear the most to give Him.

3 - He says: Go to the Centre and all divergence will vanish.

4 - He says: I am the Inspirer who is never found where you claim to find him.

5 - He says: Do submit totally to His Will and you will be liberated from all worries for/in the future.

6 - He says: Truly, His verdict is just; no one has received the right to criticise Him.

7 - He says: Understand, the one who ignores the Main Thing perishes in darkness even though he was endowed with all the power to become a son of light.

22

1 - He says: God never punishes; the fact is, your own doubts are your foes and cause trouble.

2 - He says: While you float on a sea of unconsciousness, the world will remain full of intolerable suffering.

3 - He says: Whomever stands on the threshold doesn't taste of the bliss of achievement.

4 - He says: Go before He who comes, the Expected One, the Young Son chosen, crowned and conquering.

5 - He says: Those who delay the moment to fly up towards the honey-sweet plains see their dreams becoming nightmare, their dwelling will become ice, and for a long time they will have no rescue point.

6 - He says: Truly, The drinker, the wine and the cup are one.

7 - He says: Understand, whomever abuses magic and won't have taken the time to distil the juices of wisdom will die empty of days.

23

1 - He says: When you were only a formless mass drifting in the plain of perdition, I created a perfect setting for your fulfilment. What is drawn in my plan will inevitably occur and lead you to Liberation.

2 - He says: Dissolve your doubts, close the locks of anguish, unify your life, act according to my Will and declare the religion of Freedom.

3 - He says: Focus all your attention of whatever deeds of your hand under the tall vault above your heads.

4 - He says: If you seek and take refuge in Him, with all the fibers of your being, then you will easily reach the eternal condition.

5 - He says: The Green voice is the sole source of both the Word of Ancient Folks and the Word of the New; to obey it in an unconditional fashion is what constitutes the just spiritual practice.

6 - He says: Truly, those who long for Him attach themselves to a rope that cannot be severed.

7 - He says: Understand, one's constant recollection of the Lord facilitates one's communion with His always Active Will that works for your liberation.

24

1 - He says: The Call falls upon from the vault of Heaven, but trapped in the snare you set, you do listen to it.

2 - He says: Rise above the horizon, you Galaadians, and be in harmony with the Omni-Vibration. It is through it that Creation is renewed and you will go beyond the bounds of this finite world.

3 - He says: The first being towards which one must be merciless is one's self. Pray God to strengthen you, Him who personifies for all Creation the very model of Force and Beauty.

4 - He says: May your language and tongue multiply itself by six hundred sixty six thousand times, and more, so that you can endlessly sing the glory of the First One, He who created from your ashes the cosmos submitted to the laws of His Will so that you are able to reach the Highest State.

5 - He says: He who distributes His Gifts without getting bored, He gives to the souls a strong beverage so that they may fall into a divine drunkenness sober than sobriety itself.

6 - He says: Truly, rare is mistletoe on the oaks; likewise, scarce are those who attain true wisdom.

7 - He says: Understand, there remains the right to run away when you do not reach what you wish for.

25

He says: I am not He Whom one begs with fear for salvation.

2 - He says: Cursed be the worshippers hoping for a reward in the same way traders hope for a price from selling their merchandise.

3 - He says: The helmsman that steer the ship towards the Great Shore endows those who hear and respond positively to His Call with a victory, each day, over the Fomoire with the evil eye.

4 - He says: The present errors spare you the mistakes of the future, but time is not meant to be filled with vain deeds.

5 - He says: It is only after learning how to use freedom correctly that God will grant you liberty.

6 - He says: Truly, planting occurs only after a preliminary clearing for cultivation.

7 - He says: Understand, if you walk in a direction opposite to the way shown clearly to you by He who ordained all that exists for you highest welfare, then His arm will throw you down into the dust.

26

1 - He says: The ones enjoy themselves in the dregs of society while the others land on the top of mountains. Get purified from/of all that obscure you and join me.

2 - He says: Your adversary is always right. It is surpassing your limits that you will go round him and be able to vanquish him.

3 - He says: The struggle for life is the struggle for the possession of perfection.

4 - He says: The lion doesn't eat the dog's leftovers and the work of toads is not befitting an eagle. Gods behave according to the Wish of God, but those who worship the dead and the graves toil in vain. Stop, become aware of the lamentable state in which you find yourself, utter your declaration of disapprobation and re-direct your activity having your eyes focused on the sublime heights of the Eternal Dwelling to which the Master of Masters calls you.

5 - He says: Attaining the Highest State requires a perspective in which each sees the hand of God in all things.

6 - He says: Truly, constancy and bravery will allow you to re-cover your heritage.

7 - He says: Understand, the source of just laws is in the Mighty Hand that supports and suspends the scales.

27

1 - He says: The Might acts in every moment, the Call of the Lord of Light resounds each second in the Tree. Make sure you are in unison with His Will and fly up towards the realm of total freedom and pure bliss.

2 - He say: The wise man follows the Lord of the cycle and feeds on the proclamation of the heralds that summon men and women to follow Him. On the appointed day, joining the Summoning of the Successor wisely saves time and means.

3 - He says: Splendid is the new Dawn, tower born towards your shores of sky and night. Answer that you are ready, acknowledge the Unique One, obey the Supreme Chief and work to free the Earth from the slavery in which the drifters' vain imagination keeps her.

4 - He says: The Star of the Chosen one has burst forth from the silver cloud above Creation's horizon. His Might is a flagrance of perfume, a pure gift and a triumphing peace. Penetrate in the intelligence of this emblem that has been given only to be heard and understood.

5 - He says: Submitting to God's orders leads to greatness while disobeying Him leads to misfortune.

6 - He says: Truly, the living and the dead are not similar; the living are those who say 'yes', the dead are those who say 'no' and look towards the past.

7 - He says: Understand, everything happens in due time. Today, the Morning Star of Six Hundred Sixty Six shines on the forehead of the Galaadians, those who direct their energy towards what can serve His Cause in a better fashion, those who listen to His Inspiration and come closer to the peaceful sources of His Science. Great is the blessing that is reserved for them, great is the fortune of those who recognise and acknowledge the truly excellent majesty of the First One, the Student, the Provider who spreads upon the world the beams of His luminous direction.

III. THE TREE

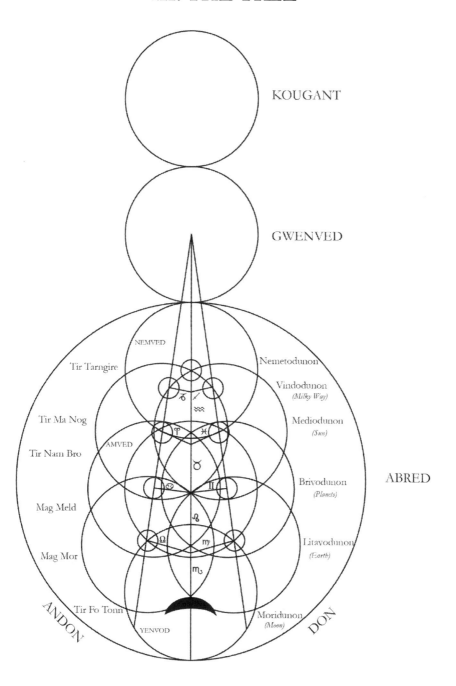

KOUGANT

GWENVED

Tir Tarngire

NEMVED

Nemetodunon

Vindodunon
(Milky Way)

Mediodunon
(Sun)

Tir Ma Nog

AMVED

Tir Nam Bro

Brivodunon
(Planets)

ABRED

Mag Meld

Mag Mor

Litavodunon
(Earth)

ANDON

Tir Fo Tonn

YENVOD

Moridunon
(Moon)

DON

On top: the sphere of KOUGANT.

Beneath: the sphere of GWENVED.

From GWENVED come the three rays that make up the TREE established in the sphere of ABRED.

ABRED consists of:

- top: the sphere of NEMVED.

- middle: the sphere of AMVED.

- bottom: the sphere of YENVED.

At the bottom left of ABRED is found ANDON, and at the bottom right resides DON.

Within the left of ABRED are found, from top to bottom:

- TIR TAIRNGIRE the Land of Promises.

- TIR NA NOG the Land of Youth.

- MAG MELD the Plain of Pleasures.

- MAG MOR the Great Plain.

- TIR FO TONN the Land under the Waves.

Within the right of ABRED, from top to bottom, are found:

- NEMETODUNON.

- VINDODUNON the Milky Way.

- MEDIODUNON the Sun.

- BRIVODUNON the Planets.

- LITAVODUNON the Earth.

- MORIDUNON the Moon.

Six spheres interpenetrate one another starting from NEMVED down to YENVED. Three to the left and three to the right.

The Tree structure starts in NEMVED emanating from the three rays born in GWENVED.

The top of the tree is the junction of the interpenetrating, in the sphere of NEMVED, of the left and right sphere just

beneath.

The Tree has four branches to the left from to bottom: Capricorn, Aries, Cancer and Libra.

The Tree has four branches to the right from to bottom: Sagittarius, Pisces, Gemini and Virgo.

The trunk between the four top branches is Aquarius.

The middle trunk separating top branches from lower branches is identified with Taurus.

The trunk between the four lower branches is identified with Leo.

The bottom trunk between the eight branches and the crescent-shaped base of the Tree, which is the intersection of the bottom

left and right sphere in YENVED, is identified with Scorpio.

IV. THE CIRCLES

1 - He says: According to the Word of the Ancient Ones, of happy memory, there are three life circles:

- The Circle of KOUGANT;

- The Circle of GWENVED;

- The Circle of ABRED.

2 - He says: The Circle of KOUGANT is the most distinguished of all, beyond which it is impossible to conceive anything, because all that exists is comprised within it.

3 - He says: In KOUGANT, the Unknowable remains hidden in His transcendence. It has always been veiled in the eternity of KOUGANT, and it will remain forever concealed from the fires and lights of creatures.

4 - He says: Nothing can be spoken about the Unknowable. He is beyond all designation and nobody has access to Him. No definition can define Him; neither name nor description can be specific about Him; no knowledge can contain Him; he does not admit neither multiplication nor change nor form; He is the Principle, beyond the one and the many; He is the hugely exalted Absolute above all.

5 - He says: The Unknowable created the Circle of GWENVED as a state of light forms of such a multitude that no number can make a census of it.

6 - He says: Truly, the light forms of GWENVED are only Sparks of the Unbearable Light that is in the Principle.

7 - He says: Understand, this happened in the beginning: One of the GWENVED's Light forms started spontaneously to meditate and contemplated himself as well as his fellow creatures. This beaming one realized that his fellow creatures and himself had a Principle different from themselves and they were powerless to know It. The Light form denied deity to both his fellow creatures and himself, and he vouched for deity as belonging to his principle.

Through this very act he was deserving to get the title of King of the High Kings of Light. It is him who is called LUG in the old annals.

That being established, He received from the Unknowable, as a privilege to the exclusion of his fellow creatures, the Divine Sap through which he became immortal and spared of the possibility of him making mistakes, alteration and annihilation.

Meanwhile, one of those Splendor Giants understood, but only partially, what Lug had comprehended. He refused to acknowledge Lug' superior station even though he was behind the King of the High Kings of Light in terms of understanding.

This Splendor Giant imagined he was equal with the Elevated one.

BRAN, so named in the old annals, started to preach rebellion around him and undertook to convert to his error many other light forms. Through this deed, Bran and those who followed him fell from their rank and became isolated in the sphere they had condensed around themselves. Such was the first origin of the circle of ABRED.

Then, it occurred that the rebellious light started to meditate and, following long reflections, the horror and despair of his situation became obvious to him. He understood that the circle of his isolation was, due to its inferior condition, bound to time and that it would end with all its content like all that is not divine and doesn't possess the mark of eternity.

Feeling regrets and blaming himself, Bran was sorry for his previous attitude. He interceded with Lug, begging the latter to forgive both him and those he had converted to his rebellion.

The Very-Generous One pardoned Bran's wrongs. Knowing that the former rebel had not been hardened by the revolt, Lug thus forgave the anterior wandering from truth, and he re-established Bran to his former position, allowing him to taste of an abundance of Divine Sap which preserved him from future mistakes and granted him also eternal life, as in the case of the other Beaming Ones who had acknowledged Lug as their Lord.

But while Bran was interceding with Lug, those who followed the rebel revolted against him, claiming nobody could prevail as all were initially equal in Being.

Lug said: 'Go before those who followed your example after listening to your words, call them and liberate them from the prison into which they fell.'

Bran leaned over them with sympathy and said: 'We were wrong in refusing to acknowledge the superiority of the Very-Glorious who is more advanced than us. I myself have regret for what I have done. You too must be sorry for what happened and then you will reach bliss and triumph.'

But they answered in unison to this speech: 'Neither you nor the other are more important than us, as we all together are the unique creation of the Unknowable.'

Through this answer, they radically darkened the core of their being. What had been a noble and luminous became a compact mass, opaque and frozen. Stuck together, they ran away to set their tents in a certain vast plain called the place of perdition. They elected a chief named BALOR by the old annals.

Bran asked: 'What can we do to help them feel sorry and return to the right path?'

'The sparks are not yet extinguished under the ice, answered Lug, I will build a world that will be like a ladder to help them go back to our sphere.'

Then the Supreme Aid projected His Breath in a three-fold melody of Power, Perfection and Harmony emitted according to three modes:

- Belonging to SLEEP, in YENVED, where are located the most hardened one.

- Belonging to MOANING, in AMVED, where one sows, cultivates and reaps.

- Belonging to SMILE, in NEMVED, where is located the Land of Promises, account of the final reintegration.

Thus, through the working of the Three-fold Energy at work, new forms came from the dark mass: they grew and increased in number in the constant ebb and flow on the Tree of Life created for the liberation of the prisoners of the Abyss.

Bran said: 'Whomever is a chief must be a bridge, as it is on account of my fault that they became lost, and so it is through me that they will be saved; consequently dispose of my life.'

Lug answered: 'It is fair that the one who was the first rebel has to wait for the return of the last of them.'

Having said that, Lug severed Bran's head and put it on top of the Tree. Since then, it has become the source of Divine Sap, the Dew of Light that irrigates the tree trunk, the branches and the foliage in ABRED.

V. THE LADY

1 - He says: May the name of the Goddess of goddesses be glorified! She is one and three and nine; it is the Mother who gives birth and make all things blossom; But Her and Her child are not identical.

2 - He says: Silently, Dana weaves behind all forms; all creatures come from her craft and trade and all return to the craft and trade while this is necessary.

3 - He says: Dana is the creating Energy, the Inexpressible Power, the Cosmic Force that supports the universe, the Great She-Magician who animates Multiplicity.

4 - He says: Dana acts in the stars as in your world, in water as in the plants, in animals as in man; She is the Mother of the Gods, alien to all birth.

5 - He says: Dana knows better than anyone what is necessary for and to each, and She caters for it in the right at the right place. Her supreme office is to cater for and activate the growth of the child of light and immortality.

6 - He says: Truly, She watches, She awaits and She goes to fetch the one who is abandoned; She directs the consciousness and leads it from illumination to illumination to the fullness of (the) light.

7 - He says: understand, Dana is the All-Might of the All-Mighty, the Flame of Delight; in Her rest letters, stanza, melodies and formula; if it was not for Her, the world would perish.

O Greatest of all Goddesses, O Dana
You who make no difference among all creatures
And for/to Whom night and day are equivalent
Make me consider men as insects and insects as men
The Whole as Nothingness.
Free me from Evil, that is to say, from the belief that something must be avoided

38

And thus, from fear and scruples.
Free me from Good, that is to say, from the belief that something may be desired
And thus, from envy, jealousy, cupidity and pride/arrogance.
Give me the freedom of the Wind.

VI. THE NWYVRE

1 - He says: It is by the working of the Secret Threefold Fire that The Supreme Artist carries out His projects.

2 - He says: This Perfume of God, this Creating Breath is the Ram-Snake of ages and of the power which goes through all things and open for itself a burning path in the abyss.

3 - He says: His Always Active Will has three aspects that are the three Spears of strength with three wicks, that is to say, electric fire, fire obtained by rubbing/friction and solar fire.

4 - He says: The Nine manifest the Three to the full and all are fundamentally One.

5 - He says: Learn in this life to fusion the Three Currents of the most redoubtable Power that man has received as a loan, for it is through the UNVANAERTAN that the AWEN can grow and that elevation becomes possible; the mastery of it grants all the powers in this world.

6 - He says: Truly, the union of the Three and his progression indicate the opening of the liberating process; beauty then enters in the obscure passages of thought, for where are united the Three then the fourth realizes the unity and mistletoe can grow on the tree.

7 - He says: Understand, the profuse and whirling Secret Fire that gives its clarity to the Sun, shoots and blazes through the depths of the universe, it is this force that watches over the roots of growth, that frees the jewel from its mud, cuts it and allows it to throw the fullness of its beaming.

VII. THE GODS OF DANA

TARANIS, ANDARTA:
- Dagodevos, Arduinna | Harp-player, Wisdom | 1 (Dragon's head), 10 (Aries), 100 (Capricorn)
- Nodons, Morrigana | Fighter, Knowledge | 4 (Mars), 40 (Moon), 400 (Neptune)
- Sukellos, Nantosuelta | Bronze-smith, Meditation | 7 (Saturn), 70 (Pallas), 700 (Cancer)

ESUS, SIRONA:
- Ogmios, Bodva | Chronicler, Understanding | 2 (Sagittarius), 20 (Pisces), 200 (Mercury)
- Medros, Matrona | Healer, Research | 5 (Vierge), 50 (Terre), 500 (Neptune)
- Smertrios, Rosmerta | Carpenter, Teaching | 8 (Gémeaux), 80 (Black Moon -Lilith), 800 (Jupiter)

BELENOS, BELISAMA:
- Kernunnos, Rigantona | Magician, Intelligence | 3 (Taurus), 30 (Aquarius), 300 (Pluto)
- Maponos, Epona | Cupbearer, Science | 6 (Uranus), 60 (Venus), 600 (Leo)
- Gobannions, Brigantia | Blacksmith, Poetry | 9 (Scorpio), 90 (Sun), 900 (Dragon's tail)

VIII. THE TRIBES OF THE GODDESS

He says: Under the aegis of the three Dynasties, there are nine tribes grouping nine Hierarchies that form the whole of the creative arms:

- - The Hierarchy of the Scepters of Wisdom, of the Tribe of Dagodevos and of the Dynasty of Taranis.

- - The Hierarchy of the Arks of Glory, of the Tribe of Ogmios and the Dynasty of Esus.

- - The Hierarchy of the Thrones of Harmony, of the Tribe of Kernunnos and of the Dynasty of Belenos.

- - The Hierarchy of the Candlesticks of Victory, of the Tribe of Nodons and of the Dynasty of Taranis.

- - The Hierarchy of the Hearts of Flame, of the Tribe of Medros and of the Dynasty of Esus.

- - The Hierarchy of the Princes of Light, of the Tribe of Maponos and of the Dynasty of Belenos.

- - The Hierarchy of the Columns of Power, of the Tribe of Sukellos and the Dynasty of Taranis.

- - The Hierarchy of the Wings of Majesty, of the Tribe of Smertrios and of the Dynasty of Esus.

- - The Hierarchy of the Regents of Splendor, of the Tribe of Gobannions and of the Tribe of Belenos.

2 - He says: The Tribes and hierarchies are always linked the ones to the others and work with awareness in the cosmos; they represent the totality of the active instrument and the result of its action.

3 - He says: It is through the Dynasties, with the Tribes and according to the correct number of the Hierarchical Entities, that the Mystery of this universe is built.

IX. THE COLORS

1 - He says: Green is the Tree of mature timber on which are produced all the marvels of Creation; in its branches, birds make their nests and men and gods have their place.

2 - He says: The Word of the Old ones, of happy memory, allocates red to Taranis, blue to Esus and yellow to Belenos.

3 - He says: Twelve are the colors of the palette covered by the Tree of the world; three and nine:

- - White is for NEMVED, Red for AMVED and Black for YENVED.
- - Above: Red and white on the left; blue and white on the right and yellow plus white in the center.
- - In the middle: Red and red on the left; blue and red on the right and yellow plus red in the center.
- - Below: Red and black on the left; blue and black on the right and yellow plus black in the center.

X. THE SCIENCES

1 - He says: To the Three Current of Energy through which the Will of the Creator spreads, correspond the three Sciences that answer the needs of those who passionately seek liberation:

-   - The Great Science of Arcanum, that is dispensed by Taranis, the force that removes obstacles with the power of gnosis and wisdom, and that is the prerogative of anyone who knows.

-   - The Great science that illuminates, that is dispensed by Esus, the force that removes obstacles with the power of devotion and contemplation, and that is the prerogative of anyone who sees.

-   - The Great Science of the sun, that is dispensed by Belenos, the force that removes obstacles with the power of synthesis and action, and that is the prerogative of anyone who acts.

2 - He says: The Great Science that is Complete gathers them all, and that is the prerogative of the KELC'HIER.

3 - He says: The Sciences do contradict one another; all lead you to the same goal and all make you perfect.

XI. THE GREAT WORK

1

1 - He says: according to the Word of the Ancient ones, of happy memory, the Great Work is the transformation of all things that are vile into things that are precious. It is the turning of the impure state into the pure state of the dark state into the luminous state. It is symbolized by lead transmuting into gold.

2 - He says: Raw material must be accepted as it exists and must be treated as it is.

3 - He says: Learn to acquire and exercise the long patience necessary to carry out the Work; be ready to sacrifice what is lesser when what is vaster is perceived.

4 - He says: The whole of man's activity must be concentrated in the sole aim to form a being of light.

5 - He says: You must neither dream nor take a rest, you must toil and reap, you must follow the path in looking up.

6 - He says: Truly, the three Victories must be won as soon as possible.

7 - He says: Understand, those who desire to succeed enter into the thickness of the Tree that is the path of life.

2

1 - He says: It is only rebellion that produces suffering and grief; peace is found behind the energies that fight against one another.

2 - He says: make peace among yourselves, do not identify yourselves with circumstances and contexts, stay firm like steel in the wound.

3 - No one has most hatred against the tree than the earth that holds it, but the time when the dog rose bush blossoms is the moment when man enters in his eternity.

4 - He says: Do not put the cauldron upon the fire when the latter is extinguished.

5 - He says: The Blacksmith goes down into the depths to find the material with which he will be able to express his craft and fashion what is beautiful.

6 - He says: Truly, only the armed hand can be used in the Great Work.

7 - He says: Understand, the overall aim can only be perceived when each king's son has access in awareness to his divine heritage.

3

1 - He says: It is in a growing fashion that souls come to know themselves.

2 - He says: The Word of the Ancient ones, of happy memory, says that the core of the doctrine is not revealed to the slaves.

It is true that it is divulged only to the good man or good woman who alone desires to hear and understand it.

3 - He says: he who has known the prison's walls goes into the lights with the eyes opened.

4 - He says: The desirable unification doesn't imply negligence towards nothing, but implies attentive care to each part so that it has the ability to contribute to the welfare of all organism.

5 - He says: Depart questing for the gold, the raven will be nourished in a virile manner and the Voice will tell you what you have to do.

6 - He says: Truly, when the mineral is melted, the gangue burns with the alloy.

7 - He says: Understand, all suffering are like the sieve/riddle in which the grain is sorted out and separated.

4

1 - He says: If you learn what the gift of life is about, then you will be initiated to the secret of love.

2 - He says: You must love everything that lives more than yourself.

3 - He says: Be one with the life of all forms, then you will enter more easily in the outer circle of He who is the origin of all things.

4 - He says: Pleasure nourishes and liberates in much the same way as suffering.

5 - He says: You must be able to blossom where God has sown you.

6 - He says: Truly, everything is permitted, for you do not know God's ways and ignore that they go through excess and error.

7 - He says: Understand, The perfection of each thing consists in surpassing one's self.

5

1 - He says: A mystery remains a mystery as long as ignorance and unbelief exist.

2 - He says: The artist separates in order to re-unite in a better fashion doesn't expect a reward. Those who do the contrary feed only on thorns.

3 - He says: The power hidden in the body, if it is genuinely known properly used, grants omniscience and liberation.

4 - He says: If from the cup three drops overflow and fall on the palm of he who holds it, then he will never go astray in his stroll in the forest of remains.

5 - He says: There is no joy comparable with the one that occurs when the Work is achieved.

6 - He says: Truly, To know doesn't suffice, as you must drink and breath the perfumes of warm reality.

7 - He says: Understand, You gain in height when you leave the low City; Gaining in height, that is to say nobility, means that something has changed in your mode of being, it implies that you are transformed and made lighter.

6

1 - He says: Treasures plunderers enjoy the Hospitality of the Generous one.

2 - He says: The sword's steel that has been transmuted into gold touched by the philosophical stone, keeps its form but cannot wound anyone.

3 - He says: The KELC'HIER knows the Gods and the forces, but he holds in his awareness and consciousness the will to surpass them.

4 - He says: whomever judges and feels pity serves the past. Forgetting the things of the past, you will advance and enlarge the channel of contact.

5 - He says: The world's harmonies were created through the Nine Words of the old wise men; by those words the harmonies are developed and interpreted.

6 - He says: Truly, understanding the secret hidden under the bark of existence is always acquired at the expense of blood.

1. 7 - He says: Understand, no science is valid if it doesn't pursue the liberation of man.

7

1 - He says: Making up with one's self is the first victory, the foundation of the work that allows the birth of the perfect form of light.

2 - He says: Be what is in every moment, and the (feeling of) separation will vanish for what-cannot-be-changed will have invaded everything.

3 - He says: The only worthy thing is the conquest of what is eternal.

4 - He says: Those who defeat the traps of the obscure citadel rise in the hierarchy of light. Those under siege rely on their discipline to get away from the grip of those who besiege.

5 - He says: Throw three drops on the incandescent blade; according to whether the elixir will have been prepared either in the red mode or in the white mode, the blade will turn red or white, internally or externally.

6 - He says: Truly, all passions and deeds must be oriented towards Him.

7 - He says: Understand, united by the link of a perfect equity, The Galaadians start their adventure on the middle path; all are armed, and all must vanquish, but necessarily in the same way.

8

1 - He says: Servitude must be used to destroy all servitude.

2 - He says: The wheel of KROUI doesn't turn like a chariot's wheel, either forward or backward; it turns in both directions at once, simultaneously.

3 - He says: Whatever direction his steed follows, the quester has only one religion and one law and that is freedom.

4 - He says: When reaching achievement, the pilgrim wandering in the night becomes the child crowned with gold entering through the door of his radiant orb.

5 - He says: You must sow your grains without counting, but if you plant a bad seed and expect a good result, then your hope is vain.

6 - He says: Truly, odd are the ways of the Great Enchanter, but he does everything for the better.

7 - He says: Understand, nothing was created at random, but with a view of the task assigned to all.

9

1 - He says: What is gross must be transmuted into something subtle; you will reach your objective by progressing towards subtler reality.

2 - He says: There is no difference between the Tree and the Great Work, for the twelve are divided up into the four, and the great transmutation finds its consummation at the top of the ascent when the gangue reveals its hidden gem, and the work of cutting and polishing is accomplished. Then the glory of the incomparable gem is displayed in its three qualities: hardness, purity and transparency.

3 - He says: The intensity of light in the world depends on the number of your brothers who are truly luminous.

4 - He says: Have faith in what you must become; this ideal will show up as it is the goal that is placed before you.

5 - He says: What is not imperfect is not an impediment, for nobody is perfect.

6 - He says: Truly, this life is the right method as you are the result of your past.

7 - He says: Understand, evil is what can be dominated and subjugated, but to which it is allowed to govern.

10

1 - He says: According to the Word of the Ancient ones, of happy memory, the Land of Promises and all its wonders is not the ultimate stage.

2 - He says: Nothing is totally deprived of beauty, consequently all things are capable of giving you joy.

3 - He says: Experience lived on the three age-less and fault-less hills is the secret of the transposed cruciform.

4 - He says: All is wed exactly by He who plants, waters and gives growth.

5 - He says: Remain stable and go forwards without wearing down.

6 - He says: Truly, the wealth of heaven is poured on to anyone who gives.

7 - He says: Understand, punishment is the transmutation of former errors.

11

1 - He says: The perfect eye is the organ by which the Creator's energy is poured towards His instruments of service.

2 - He says: Do not maintain separation, but draw from yourselves a light that cannot perish. Sterile ascetic persons' late regrets will remain vain.

3 - He says: It is incumbent upon the superior man to seek what is only possible of being attained.

4 - He says: The flight is done in/with the point that is rising, the fusion is accomplished in/with the cone.

5 - He says: No material will be left without purification.

6 - He says: Truly, You choices carry you along and you are the fruit of your works.

7 - He says: Understand, if today you worry for the morrow, you lose track of the present day that runs away with your precious life.

12

1 - He says: The ascent must be constant with what is offered in each moment by the totality of things.

2 - He says: What has been sown in the past will bear fruit in this life if the soil is appropriate.

3 - He says: Freedom is always shaped in the contact with another freedom.

4 - He says: The Possessor of Treasures must be invoked whenever there is a booty.

5 - He says: Throw yourselves into His inferno and dance with the flames as it is a good mean to cleanse the scoria.

6 - He says: Truly, the armed hand is an empty hand.

7 - He says: Understand, it would be vain to claim to strip the bark from the tree before the time of maturity.

13

1 - He says: The elimination of the ego is the first remedy to guarantee your liberation from causal binding.

2 - He says: To pray for one's self is the expression of the most abject selfishness. Pray for all, for the most restricted is included in the greater whole, and both man's fulfilment and the nature of his liberation occur only in correlation with the greater form of existence in ABRED in which are located your infinite forms.

3 - He says: Follow the shining thread spun by the ermine across this world in which the Galaadians build an inviolate masterpiece.

4 - He says: All blade that serves its master is good, and all crime has its beauty and its price.

5 - He says: A slave cannot elaborate any individuality, and never has freedom taken root in a place inhabited by sadness. But in the dwelling that renews the nobility of the noble man, the Cup circulates from the hands of adolescent having submitted time to their own yoke.

6 - He says: Truly, the form is the vine, the soul is the wine.

7 - He says: Understand, you will flower like a vine, your perfume will give out a flagrance and your flowers will yield rich and weighty grapevine.

14

1 - He says: Each stage of the re-ascent has been forecast along various paths fitting your different natures.

2 - He says: Misery in human life is due to ignorance, but any kind of ignorance; liberation is due to science, but not any kind of science. The true liberating science attracts man towards the zenith, where shines the highest of all lights.

3 - He says: See His hand in everything and take the road that leads to the source of contentment.

4 - He says: In the radiant beauty of and the geometry of the dodecahedron-like diamond resides the glory of the final transmutation.

5 - He says: The ladder must be stepped in different fashions until it disappears in the exact awareness and consciousness of things.

6 - He says: Truly, only doubt in the heart of man is an impenetrable veil.

7 - He says: Understand, Each step on the Earth must be like a prayer.

15

1 - He says: Why do you desire a thing you are not able to possess? You can only rise to the extent of your capacity. You reach the top only gradually.

2 - He says: The delinquent seekers who do not understand the cause of the created world lose sleep and rest for ever.

3 - He says: Contain and define your desire, invoke and focus your power, and the thing will be done in a flash.

4 - He says: The act that put an end to life is always done by your hands.

5 - He says: Life is huge; what is past and what is to come are hidden in it.

6 - He says: Truly, anyone who wastes his or her life feeds on his or her own blood.

7 - He says: Understand, he who works on the dissection of his own self travails on a favorable soil.

16

1 - He says: The more a form is free from opaqueness, the more complete is its presence to itself.

2 - He says: The Kingdom is within you and in everything; it is inside and outside, like the flavor sweetened with sugar is in each point of the sugar cube.

3 - He says: Attachment, but not the deed, makes you unhappy; see things as they are and towards the higher and highest level.

4 - He says: The leaf, however green it is, shivers and trembles, then turns yellow and ends up falling on to the ground; in the same way, you are perishable here. Knowing that Death is inevitable, take to take advantage of it.

5 - He says: The rule is to be always present; do not worry about the rest.

6 - He says: Truly, , the spirit that has taken its leap towards the Divine is not bound by any obligation.

7 - He says: Understand, you have to be born many times.

17

1 - He says: If one loses the capital that is this life, one will be able to compensate for it only in the other life, in the beyond.

2 - He says: You are three in one. The transformation of crude stones into living rock can only be accomplished when the TWO join with the THIRD in the FOURTH.

3 - He says: No more than the child is born in this world wishes to re-enter the maternal womb, so no more he who leaves this sphere to go the higher planes wishes to return here-below.

4 - He says: The master resides in the servant, but do think the servant is the master.

5 - He says: God does all things for the better. Be reconciled with the lot God has chosen for you.

6 - He says: Truly, the intelligent artist eliminates the negative desires and uses the positive wishes to perfect himself.

7 - He says: Understand, as your transmutation develops and your spiritual degree rises, your body of light is perfected.

18

1 - He says: He is insane who believes to be not responsible for the misfortune of others; he himself soon starts to be sinking into affliction.

2 - He says: The constant recollection of the goal allows one to always find again a mean to re-join the good lost track.

3 - He says: The ordeals of each are reckoned to allow you to acquire the qualities necessary for your development.

4 - He says: All the circumstances and contexts in which God put yourself possess their advantages, you only have to be aware of it.

5 - He says: In the crossing of the Abyss, it is not possible to live to the half, you must be fully engaged /in with and in complete acceptance of the condition that is assigned to you.

6 - He says: Truly, the Galaadian is not afraid of confronting the different forms of armor and bloody struggle, he breathes freely and lives fully without regretting the past and free from any anxiety concerning the future.

7 - He says: Understand, everything is possible in the mixed region.

19

1 - He says: Rise! Come out of the cold shroud of your limitations, fly off and dance with the artists in the Tree.

2 - He says: The liberated soul considers all things as an opportunity for rejoicing.

3 - He says: trim and polish up the granite until reach of the complete perfection of the shining diamond, radiant, rendered brilliant by all its fires in its beautiful light.

4 - He says: The constant repetition of the efficient formula is, in this cycles, the easiest and the best mean to obtain liberation and achieve your highest Self.

5 - He says: On the abrupt spiralling path, keep watch on your steed so that it doesn't stumble.

6 - He says: Truly, sin is restriction; therefore I will have no pity for those who hesitate, but I will the crown of life for the others.

7 - He says: Understand, the only sensible thing is to confront difficulties and to conquer them in this life and in this body.

20

1 - He says: Hard, noble, free and victorious are the Celts who haul themselves up on the summits of greatness and transcend the trials of life through the constant flux and reflux of life where the soul is forged and quenched.

2 - He says: Utopia decrees that in the bottom of a pit the sky appears as big as the lid of a pot of soup.

3 - He says: In the lower circles, you were sadly moaning and were hardly sheltered from cold and hunger when you were pulling wagons, carts and ploughs. Here, bitterness and stench did not open your eyes.

4 - He says: The Galaadian takes refuge in the storm and doesn't stay in a godforsaken hole.

5 - He says: Regenerate yourselves in order to re-enter the ancient abode of bliss.

6 - He says: Truly, he who of beauty beholds only one aspect doesn't possess the right vision.

7 - He says: Understand, this beauty that is luminous is the one of your true being.

21

1 - He says: Do not throw life to the wind, for as it you are passing. It is here and now that man's task must be accomplished.

2 - He says: The Tree with the branches [or 'shoots'] that bears fruits twelve times in the year grows so that the forest is flagrant and gets green again.

3 - He says: Good is what fills you up and fulfils you, bad is what destroys you. Awake to yourself and seek what never perishes.

4 - He says: If a man who seriously study the way of/to liberation questions you three times, answer only once without him begging you, but also without useless words.

5 - He says: Through works and self- discipline, Galaadians sharpen the shining sword with which they make their way through

towards what is immortal.

6 - He says: Truly, no-one is excluded and no-one runs away from the satisfaction that is expected by and from existence.

7 - He says: Understand, the crucible is the very Gold when the Stone turns into a Tree.

22

1 - He says: He who has conquered the Grail possesses the secret of cheerful death.

2 - He says: The pleasures of life strengthen the vigor of men towards the difficult tasks.

3 - He says: This band of players on the chessboard accept in advance what will falls to them, they have chosen to risk their life in adventure, they fight without rest and have turned war into a time of safety in their lives.

4 - He says: Temple in which the Power is manifested, a body is necessary for/to Art. Misfortune to the prince who doesn't see beauty in the young man with curled hair and in the maiden with golden hair!

5 - He says: When each avenue has been explored without yielding any result, it is legal to take the sword; but anyone who wages war without motivation will perish by his own weapons.

6 - He says: Truly, gain and loss are only one.

7 - He says: Understand, he who practices the law of Freedom executes things with precision and exactness.

23

1 - He says: As long as your skulls will not be turned into cup, the fire that you have lit will not burn.

2 - He says: Forget your fears and your bogus hopes; kill the other's certitude and strike the one who hit you; Prepare yourself for battle and remove who are clumsy in fighting face to face.

3 - He says: According to the Word of the Ancient ones, of happy memory, there are four festivals and reserved beverages; but it is only when the highest of the three warlike desires will practised and tested in the world floods of milk and honey will come out of rivers, and the Moon, re-established in her original state, will become a magnificent crown who feel younger.

4 - He says: As the eagle wandering in the forest and that, as soon as dawn, eats its preys who fell due to the bird's cunning, so you mustn't lose your prey until your appetite is satisfied.

5 - He says: There are sure means to satisfy all desires. When the wishes held in one's heart have been realised, one who is mortal becomes immortal.

6 - He says: Truly, Each victim who atones for old crimes is guilty.

7 - He says: Understand, To advise both hardness and softness is good, but if you kill the viper and spare its little ones, then you are not wise. Feel no pity towards the adversary who can be killed, but he would show no pity if you were in his position.

24

1 - He says: Position yourself in the center of the ring and let the spontaneous fulfilment of things take place. Your only wealth is to be a man or a woman of the present; the insane ceaselessly steps forth and steps back.

2 - He says: The concentration of the scattered beams of the Secret Fire, in accordance with the chosen path with the keys of the sound, is absolutely indispensable to the progress of the perfect realization of the Great Work.

3 - He says: Spiritualize your works, direct yourself towards Him, consciously join your will with God's own.

4 - He says: Polish the granite of all its bony aspects, and carve on it My Seal with immortal letters.

5 - He says: In each plane resounds a different note, but the seventh one swallows all the others.

6 - He says: Truly, Divine Music resounds in each of you; it is in harmony with it that the world is regulated.

7 - He says: Understand, God helps those who help themselves. Become aware of the Divine Plan, shed away all skepticism and get in harmony with the Supreme Song that provides the essence of joy and freedom.

25

1 - He says: Winning over one's self is winning over the limited world.

2 - He says: Work ceaselessly on your real progress and development. It is in forcing one's naturalness, it is in willing to do more that intelligence finds out its resources.

3 - He says: Long was your journey through many births, deaths and rebirths. It is indispensable to day to hit with the axe at the root of error in order to sever the bad causes.

4 - He says: Duality must be surpassed. Then the three go to four and realise the Supreme Unification of the Real.

5 - He says: In the still of the heart, through the ATHANOR of affliction, by saying yes and the consequent submission, you will seek and find the true Stone of the Wise ones.

6 - He says: Truly, when the seven initiations are taken, man can settle in the center and acts as a supplier of divine energy in all directions.

7 - He says: Understand, There is no alternative to freedom or slavery. The art that transforms darkness into light and slavery into freedom is a noble and special art.

26

1 - He says: If you draw from evil a surplus of life, suffering will be able to help you learn the suitable perfumes.

2 - He says: There are no vain and lost efforts and nothing is to be rejected in the quest for long life.

3 - He says: It is in the center of the plateaux, by means of the wheel, that the true perspective and the right action can be correctly glimpsed and anticipated.

4 - He says: Withdraw in the silence and get attuned to the whole. Then depart for a new adventure. To keep to the chosen path and the union of opposites will lead the seeker to the illuminated summit in the joy of proven success.

5 - He says: Through fusion and mixing, applying his creative and creating free will, the magician re-arranges chaos so that beauty can shine.

6 - He says: Truly, good is what purifies and perfects the soul, whereas evil is what weakens and draws the soul away from God.

7 - He says: Understand, action and intention are linked.

27

1 - He says: He who has found his master has only to let his growth take place. May you have no other master but Him, He who knows All, generosity itself.

2 - He says: The condition of all that is opaque and dense is the tendency to go down; the condition of all that is subtle is to rise, the tendency to go up. Through the putting into practice of the secret of transforming the venom into nectar, the purest and the most subtle in the root of the Tree ascends until it becomes a flower.

3 - He says: The world is perfectly suited to the role it must fulfil. You must work in it following the rules of what must be done, rejecting what must not be done, pursuing without respite your superior own good.

4 - He says: This song that elevates and dilates is played on strings made with your own nerves tightened on the harp of the body.

5 - He says: Consent to the temporary disagreements keeping in mind the future glory that will dissolve the clouds of the present time.

6 - He says: Truly, the purity of cups stems from the purity of the hidden meaning.

7 - He says: Understand, air attracts the Inner Fire at the junction of the three; by this mean one commits oneself and starts on the path of/to liberation, but the forces must be knotted permanently so that subsist this deliverance.

28

1 - He says: The creator of one's self is always looking for new horizons; he governs his own life and develops his possibilities in awareness.

2 - He says: Learn to remain silent, calm and fearless, in the high region where the sea surrounds the rock but doesn't occupy it.

3 - He says: The domain of training is life in the world and its particular circumstances.

4 - He says: Take advantage of each second to seek for the antidote.

5 - He says: If pleasure is short, suffering will not be able to have a hold on you.

6 - He says: Truly, when the free soul commands instead of praying or begging, all that she decides is immediately realized.

7 - He says: Understand, when the Kelc'hier has attained his highest aim, he drinks the milk tasting like ecstasy honey from the Vessel of the Cup-bearer.

29

1 - He says: Getting over limitations doesn't mean to take short-cuts; the consequences of an abrupt ascent are always perilous.

2 - He says: The dry wood is not equal to the green wood, but nothing is illegitimate for in reality both are one and the same thing.

3 - He says: Anyone who doesn't possess self-control is under the sign of his own AWEN; if he is acting in all things following a rising direction, he will not be able to grow weaker.

4 - He says: the only loss to be feared is the one of the awareness of the beginning and the end.

5 - He says: He or she who loves a creature for its beauty really loves only God, for He is the Beautiful-Being.

6 - He says: Truly, The Divine can only be found out in the sanctuary of your devotion.

7 - He says: Understand, when the branches become tender and the leaves are growing, then you know that Summer is close, but the tree can only grow and become venerable if its wood is worthless in the eye of the carpenter.

30

1 - He says: He who (asks) questions is mistaken; may he be cursed he who deprives my sword of blood.

2 - He says: Life consists of walking the way leading from the seed to the fruit.

3 - He says: It is a matter of using to the best the forces that are active and acting in this universe

4 - He says: The Grail has been carried by three tables, one being square one, the other being biquadrate and the last being round; the latter is Merlin's table. The total of their surface is six and its glory is twenty-one.

5 - He says: All the activities of the man who ignore the reason and meaning of his existence are bad.

6 - He says: Truly, man is the operator, the operated material and the crucible in which he works.

7 - He says: Understand, Success in not only dependent on the formula, but also on the one who utters it.

31

1 - He says: The great secret consists in putting theory to the test; but your time is short, that is why it is advised to tighten only one yoke.

2 - He says: Unfulfilled desires contribute to the growth of the flowers of illusion.

3 - He says: You are stronger and richer than you believe yourself to be, but humility is necessary as well as forgetting one's self if one wants to build properly and correctly.

4 - He says: Your body is the boat carrying you to the other shore of the ocean of life; make sure your mortal coal doesn't become the food of the wolf.

5 - He says: For those who strive to surpass themselves, the perfect active unification can alone guarantee the complete the transformation.

6 - He says: Truly, the gift poured by the Cup is not only the beverage of ecstasy and inspiration, not only that wave that flows but doesn't wet the hand, but it is also this reserved perfume which curls inter-mingle beyond the bark.

7 - He says: Understand, a king's son proclaims the religion of freedom; he must not die fearful in his heart, but with joy and boldness.

32

1 - He says: Harmony, peace and freedom can only blossom in the realization of the inner unity of all life, as well as in the outer expression of this same life.

2 - He says: Joy is what one experiences when one is conform to one's destiny.

3 - He says: The whole of Nature draws us towards perfection; but take care of your weapons, keep pure the four elements that is to say, air, fire, water and earth; keep the powder dry and watch.

4 - He says: All will die and all will change. You must not weep for any creature for what can you do against what is inevitable? All is as it had to be.

5 - He says: Seek what is at the highest, you will reach what is the highest.

6 - He says: Truly, a being feeds only on its root.

7 - He says: Understand, it is time for you to climb higher steps, like a grown eagle whose wings, now in their full size, stretch towards nobleness in the heights of a perfect life.

33

1 - He says: The goal of the Great Work is bringing all that is alive to the plenitude of its achievement.

2 - He says: Threefold is this vision of God on the path leading to happiness, freedom and immortality.

3 - He says: Nine beams long ago were born of the Omni-vibration; anyone who today knows those nine rays can speak with Vigor.

4 - He says: All moments are good to get a king with a queen, but the knowledge of the correct position of the fire on the altar is the essential key.

5 - He says: The many-sided Artist's Will governs the world, It is all Gods and Goddesses, the Three Currents, the nine beams and the twenty-seven mighty subtle waves.

6 - He says: Truly, the Dragon is four and it takes over three.

7 - Understand: Through surrendering to God's Will, you get away from secondary roads and you rapidly reach without mishap the highest planes.

34

1 - He says: One can never explain the apple's taste to anyone who has never tasted it; likewise, the supreme state goes beyond every description.

2 - He says: Perfection comes through right work and a firm will (power). When scoria are melted and lead bit are transmuted, you will be elevated within Splendor.

3 - He says: Lower elements are put back in the forge and on the anvil before being turned into new ploughshare.

4 - He says: Seek neither poverty nor wealth; matters only the necessary car; who can, heavily burdened, climb the Tree?

5 - He says: The true hero is anyone who knows how to dare and die in order to be acquainted with the ultimate reality.

6 - He says: Truly, it is possible for wise souls to hasten the Great Work, but not everything is dependent on the individual effort.

7 - He says: Understand, on the path that leads to the Heart of the universe, all is necessary, i.e. depths, plains and summits.

35

1 - He says: Through a free and simple life, focused entirely on God, you receive inspiration and light.

2 - He says: Things that are not in their place are agitated but when they find their place, they remain calm and rest.

3 - He says: Anyone whose ear remains open only to error remains a slave.

4 - He says: After what is difficult comes what is easy; is obscure what doesn't need to be clear.

5 - He says: Where water, earth, fire and air are united is the place proper to accomplish the magical work. Notice the colors of the pulsating material, utter the words that combine, and put the form on the right path.

6 - He says: Truly, anyone who is on the right track sees his strength increasing with each step he takes.

7 - He says: Understand, the mystery of life is concealed within the biggest circle.

36

1 - He says: Weakness, defeat and captivity must be experienced like victory, triumph and liberation.

2 - He says: If you wish to gain, you must be able to lose; If you wish to keep, you must be able to detach; if you wish to conserve, you must be able to give up. Each step forwards to the spiritual aim must always be paid for, and the price is in abandoning what, until then, was loved.

3 - He says: What has been done and made by yourself, for yourself and for the whole, will really serve to your benefit.

4 - He says: You must extract the sublet organism from the dark element, through transmutation by mean of fire, but make sure that the flame in the heart is not extinguished under ashes.

5 - He says: The remedy that is suitable for the present days is not the one needed to heal the ills of former ages.

6 - He says: Truly, the central pillar, way from/of multiplicity to/wards unity, is the luminous gain of/to anyone who can see, can work and can climb.

7 - He says: Understand, stages are made of pure vision, but also of travail and struggle; they are frantic and exhausting clings before turning into calming ecstasy.

37

1 - He says: Ripple of wisdom newly retrieved, transient convictions fall one after the other, big fears go away, sufferings leave you alone.

2 - He says: When this body prone to corruption has put on the clothes of incorruptibility, when this mortal coal has put on the dress of immortality, death is engulfed in victory and the expected benefit is fully obtained.

3 - He says: Associate God with your works, He will inspire you and you will progress rapidly in the domains that you desire.

4 - He says: You must forge your own weapons before succeeding and winning (in) the struggle.

5 - He says: It is through total freedom, true knowledge and right deed that you reach the Higher Self.

6 - He says: Truly, nothing is an obstacle, everything can be helpful, all things can be a mean to liberation. The Lord thinks of and about you in all places; therefore there is no need to fear anything.

7 - He says: Understand, insofar as you give [or: in/to the full extent in which you give], you join yourself with the Infinite.

38

1 - He says: Through the fusion and the cleansing of the black stone, and through the judicious projection of elixirs, granite becomes glass, glass becomes crystal, crystal becomes diamond, and the soul reaches her perfect form in the surpassing of the states.

2 - He says: Injustice is necessary to man in the same way as goad has to be used when dealing with oxen.

3 - He says: When you reach the top the lights converge; then what was without repose, wild like a stormy sea, becomes calm and silent.

4 - He says: Anyone who aspires to be filled must establish the void within himself.

5 - He says: Anything that can be done without a wage brings advantage to the righteous and detriment to the nasty fellow.

6 - He says: Truly, the path leading to the realization of the Divine is an easy one; but the success always awaits those who persevere and can win over obstacles and difficulties.

7 - He says: Understand, life is a constant churning and you are totally engaged in it. There are no stupid events, there are only silly people; today's wrong steps prevent tomorrow's distractions and misdirection.

39

1 - He says: To love those who love you bring only a meagre reward. The highest form of love doesn't have the desire for reciprocity.

2 - He says: Take the Cup of life with the hand of trust, then drink from it first and give an opportunity of drinking for those who advance.

3 - He says: He who will have realized his hopes will not take from Earth against his will, he will depart with joy in his heart.

4 - He says: The three-in-one knowledge brings the Kelc'hier to the realization of all harmonies. Through this accomplishment, he attains the plane of light, moves on the top and remains.

5 - He says: Do not stop so that you can drink plenty of the mead of immortality, so that you can enter the Kingdom in which dwell forever the light made of undying beauty, the faultless ecstasy and the pure bliss.

6 - He says: Truly, he who finds by himself where to put his feet on the steps of the ladder is walking firmly on the right track.

7 - He says: Understand, the stones of ice were cut by the three words of the Creator without the occurrence of any splinter flying off.

40

1 - He says: Truths go unheeded for those who don't live them organically.

2 - He says: The bard who content with only the speeches will never reach the superior stations.

3 - He says: Being a winged dragon against the forces of obscurity, the KELC'HIER cannot make a foolish mistake, he acts with great skill and doesn't run in all directions obeying the impulses of a superficial lower self.

4 - He says: Whatever the means used, when the Fires are knotted and when the UNVANAERTAN vibrates, you meet with the Will of the Lord of Light and all spiritual efforts are crowned with success.

5 - He says: Wisdom constantly receives the influence from above and give spirituality to below.

6 - He says: Truly, he who is at war with himself is at peace with his fellow men.

7 - He says: Understand, wrong penalties and wrong sorrows degrade but right torments keep you in the high region.

41

1 - He says: Put on the steel armor, go near the golden altar, fill yourself with strength to wage warfare for the Lord of Light and destroy the foes that devastate the harvests.

2 - He says: The present is bearer of absolute; there, man finds his true face and is able to live his part of eternity.

3 - He says: The living balm of high rejoicing heals the wounds on the king's thigh in thwarted the sucking trick of the Moon. Splendid are the jewels, and the stones that then spring in the heart of the Rose are incomparable.

4 - He says: Let God's Hand act upon you, and you will become tall and fruitful trees.

5 - He says: Run, like the thirsty stag, until you come across the fountain of the waters of life; unite then with life and do not be cut off from it.

6 - Truly, he who follows God's advises sees the opening of this understanding, and he leaves the pit; he who doesn't heed the divine counsels goes back to the bottom of the pit until he starts to understand.

7 - He says: Understand, female upon male, and then male upon female, each one of you seals their own destiny and the stars sing the song of eternal bliss.

42

1 - He says: Things are at the same time in many planes at once, but the truth is simple, what is indispensable is easy.

2 - He says: After having brandished his spear in such a way that the two edges join up, the Kelc'hier attaches himself to the pillar so that he doesn't die either sitting or lying down.

3 - He says: All things are entangled in the interlacing of suffering and joy, and nothing comes back twice.

4 - He says: Live fully the way of life that suits your desires, without forgetting that it is vain to wish to seize a branch that is beyond your reach.

5 - He says: There are signs and clues to get from all things, a lesson to receive from stones and plants streams and stars, sun, moon, and all that exists.

6 - He says: Truly, it is with granite and all the attributes inherent in granite that the Grail castle must be constructed in accordance with the model.

7 - He says: Understand, where the mind is without fear and knowledge is free, new melodies spring from the heart with the wonders of old words, and the harp of ancient days sings a new world for the subtle ears.

43

1 - He says: the work is often darkened with faults like fire is obscured with smoke, and it is also more difficult when the predestined element is found in small amounts; but when the time of perfection comes, then imperfection must disappear.

2 - He says: Joy and the feeling of unity with all that lives is a sign promising progress towards liberation.

3 - He says: All that is mentally visualized must be experienced by the body.

4 - He says: Having obtained true liberation, the Kelc'hier perceives all things concealed in the murmur of the Tree's leaves and help others on the spiritual path.

5 - He says: Do not question beyond the Unknowable beyond which there is nothing anymore to ask.

6 - He says: Truly, he who will have endured until the end will be said.

7 - He says: Understand, you must grow until the time of your death.

44

1 - He says: Meditate constantly on the Creator's works and be and continual communion with Him through the medium of His Presence in all things.

2 - He says: To have trust in God is not an excuse to indulge in idleness; you need at the same time to possess a tireless aspiration and you must persistently reject all that is an obstacle to the truth.

3 - He says: Co-ordinating all their deeds and impressions into a perfect harmonic whole, the Paladins march like trees at the advanced time.

4 - He says: The vision of God is nothing else but feeling and realizing His Presence in yourself and all around you; this Presence and His all-penetrating Breath bring about the growth of and dissolution of all things in Abred.

5 - He says: Do possess the sincere and ardent wish to realize your immortal nature if you want to attain perfect freedom and eternal bliss.

6 - He says: Truly, it is a matter of reaching the right head in which the sap gives its fruit and where the long eye makes one sees what has to be seen.

7 - He says: Understand, no-one can claim to quest in the right way if one rejects one's shadow.

45

1 - He says: In all his adventures, the quester passes and doesn't stop. Practicing the Law of Freedom, he gains the ability to travel through the nine gates in the cosmic spaces, enjoying, when a halt occurs, an endless bliss in the dwelling of the Hospitaller.

2 - He says: Do not look behind; bow before He who is the origin of the powers of and in your life and He makes everything new and new things in the moment.

3 - He says: Those who strive to be perfect climb the Tree as if it was a ladder. As you reach summit after summit, then you see clearly how much remains to be done in order to acquire this vision which, alone, will give you an undying contentment now and at the time of your death.

4 - He says: Ceaselessly hammered and constantly beaten, the anvil of GABANNIONS remains still. Learn from both patience and endurance, contemplating and practicing the right teachings.

5 - He says: He who deals directly with the source from which he comes reaches the end of his journey.

6 - He says: Truly, freedom is attained when man does what he does without looking ahead or behind.

7 - He says: Understand, I have thrown into the universe a Fire which beams are directed towards the bottom; may they sink profoundly within you until the ultimate arson that will burn the cosmos in liberating the strong and invincible sons of the Infinite.

XII. PRAISING THE GREEN INITIATOR

Say:

O shining Tree, in the branches of which are entangled all the inhabited lands,

Lively Tree of abundance, receptacle of all seeds and of all foods,

May its fruits give us a perfect enjoyment!

Tree of Wealth, saving creation of the King of High-Kings,

Precious wood that transforms and changes our fading away,

May we blossom again with its flowers!

Solid axis planted by the Teacher,

Mighty Tutor and firm support of ABRED,

Misfortune to those who deprive themselves of the coolness of its foliage, they are lost in error and confusion.

Happy are those who have found hospitality in the wonder of is green shadow, and who belong to those who dance in it!

Pillar of resurrection, unification of the world's horizons,

Fountain of Health that comes from this Power come to us with the Gods,

Great Tree of Life from which comes the Dew of Light,

May it take us high above so that we may drink to the full the incomparable mead in the Cup of eternal glory!

May it strengthen us in the dangers we experience!

May it be an effective shield in our combats!

May we through Him re-conquer freedom, immortality and bliss.

XIII. THE ALPHABET

Letter	Number		Number	Tree
B	2		2	Birch
L	3		14	Elm
N	4		16	Ash
F	5		6	Alder
S	6		20	Willow
H	7		8	Hawthorn
D	8		4	Oak
T	9		21	Beech tree
K	10		3	Hazel tree
CH	20		9	Holly
M	30		15	Vine
G	40		7	Creeper
P	50		18	Juniper
Z	60		25	Apple tree
R	70		19	Elederberry
C'H	80		10	Sloe tree
Y	90		12	Rowan
J	100		13	Gorse
V	200		23	Lime tree
W	300		24	Box tree
A	400		1	Pine tree
O	500		17	Broom
U	600		22	Heather
E	700		5	Aspen
I	800		11	Yew tree
	900			

XIV. THE SERIES

Letter T
Oghamic value: 9
Bardic value: 21
Zodiacal correspondence: Scorpio
Plant correspondence: Beach

1. He says: "There is nothing more, nothing less than the Only Necessity which is Death, the Father of sorrows."

Letter A
Oghamic value: 400
Bardic value: 1
Zodiacal correspondence: Balance
Plant correspondence: Pine

2. He says: "There are two oxen hitched up to a shell. They pull and they expire."

Letter F
Oghamic value: 5
Bardic value: 6
Zodiacal correspondence: Virgo
Plant correspondence: Alder

3. He says: "There are three parts in the world; three commencement and three ends for man and for tree: three marvellous realms with golden fruits, bright flowers and laughing children."

Letter U
Oghamic value: 600
Bardic value: 22
Zodiacal correspondence: Leo
Plant correspondence: Heather

4. He says: "There are four stones to sharp for the Heroes's swords."

Letter E
Oghamic value: 700
Bardic value: 5
Zodiacal correspondence: Cancer
Plant correspondence: Aspen

5. He says: "There are five Earth zones, five terrestrial zones, five stones on our sister."

Letter D
Oghamic value: 8
Bardic value: 4
Zodiacal correspondence: Gemini
Plant correspondence: Oak

6. He says: "There are four children of wax invigorated by the Moon; six plants in the cauldron; one dwarf who blends the beverage, his little finger is in his mouth."

Letter L
Oghamic value: 3
Bardic value: 14
Zodiacal correspondence: Taurus
Plant correspondence: Elm

7. He says: "There are seven suns and seven moons, seven planets including the Hen, seven elements with the Floor of the Air."

Letter K
Oghamic value: 10

Bardic value: 3
Zodiacal correspondence: Aries
Plant correspondence: Hazelnut Tree

8. He says: "There are eight blowing winds; eight fires with the Father Fire lit in May on the battle mount; eight stained heifers grazing in the Isle of Sein, the isle of Dana. The eight heifers of the Lady."

Letter CH
Oghamic value: 20
Bardic value: 9
Zodiacal correspondence: Pisces
Plant correspondence: Holly

9. He says: "There are nine white hands on the Area Table near the tower, and nine mothers shedding tears: nine korrigans dancing around the fountain below the Moon. Nine woollen robes-dressed korrigans with flower in their hair. The female boar and the nine little boars under the apple tree; the old boar's disciples."

Letter M
Oghamic value: 30
Bardic value: 15
Zodiacal correspondence: Aquarius
Plant correspondence: Vine

10. He says: "There are ten foe warships against the Venete people; Venete men prepare for battle."

Letter J
Oghamic value: 100
Bardic value: 13
Zodiacal correspondence: Capricorn
Plant correspondence: Gorse

11. He says: "There are eleven broken swords-bearer priests among the Venete people; eleven wounded priests wearing blood-stained robes. From three hundred ones, only eleven ones with their Hazel wand."

Letter B
Oghamic value: 2
Bardic value: 2
Zodiacal correspondence: Sagittarius
Plant correspondence: Birch

12. He says: "Twelve months, twelve-star signs. The last but one throws its arrow and the twelve are at war among themselves. The beautiful cow, black and white with her star-ornamented forehead, comes out of the Forest of the corpses; blood streaming. The cow lowers herself, her head held proudly high. The trumpet rings. It is thundering. the rain streams. The wind blows. Nothing will remain."

XV. THE TRIADS

1

Letter: *See Chapter XIII*
Oghamic value: 1
Astrological correspondence: Caput Draconis (The head of dragon)

1. He says: There are three wheels that have put the Gods to the test:

- The turning wheel, stained with the blood of braves,
- The rowing wheel, stained with the blood of seers,
- The flying wheel, stained with the blood of watchers.

2. He says: There are three gifts for the hero:

- The gift of hearing,
- The gift of seeing,
- The gift of judging.

3. He says: There are three horns guarded by the many-shapes King of all:

- The horn of combat,
- The horn of fertility,
- The horn of plenty.

2

Letter: P
Oghamic value: 50
Bardic value: 18
Astrological correspondence: Earth
Plant correspondence: Juniper

1. He says: There are three heads on the Old Woman:

- A smiling head.
- A weeping head.
- A laughing head.

2. He says: There are three paths in the forest of remains [spoils]:

- A preparation path.
- A development path.
- A ending path.

3. He says: There are three curtains before the entrance of the citadel:

- A fire curtain.
- An ice curtain.
- A fog curtain.

3

Letter: *See Chapter XIII*
Oghamic value: 900
Astrological correspondence: Cauda Draconis (The Dragon's tail)

1- He says: There are tree standards for the ravagers of the valley of the fomoire:

- The standard of trust and confidence.
- The standard of ardour.
- The standard of consolidation.

2- He says: There are three dissolution in the receptacle of perfumes:

- The anterior envelope.
- The ulterior edifice.
- The filter at the junction.

3- He says: There are three crowns for the wise one.

- A crown of victory.
- A crown of songs.
- A crown of fullness.

XVI. THE BRANCHES

Letter: N
Oghamic value: 4
Bardic value: 16
Astrological correspondence: Mars
Plant correspondence: Ash Tree

1. He says: The flame doesn't spare the dry twigs: the flash of lightning is not afraid to fall. But one cannot win a battle without the presence of a king. On the red and holy path, the brave one is a complete two-edged sword: existence is for him a stone to be sharpened. Become keener so that your hit is stronger.

Letter: S
Oghamic value: 6
Bardic value: 20
Astrological correspondence: Uranus
Plant correspondence: Willow tree

2. He says: Material science is the comment of/on the world of appearances, it gains by earth and water. Spiritual science leads one to the stage of ecstasy, it gains by air and fire (But making more thirsty those who are thirsty is good). When from the abyss generation you will reach the top, undo the goatskin in the high chamber of light and pour the pure gift of the life-giving wave in the space beyond your shore.

Letter H
Oghamic value: 7
Bardic value: 8
Astrological correspondence: Saturn
Plant correspondence: Hawthorn

3. He says: Retreat/retirement is the beginning; company is the end. Wisdom knows to undo the knots of things. But if you have your feet

bound to the chains of time, you die without advancing. Draw a circle of power around you, beat the mountain with your mallet, and draw from the earth all the jewels that she conceals.

Letter: G
Oghamic value: 40
Bardic value: 7
Astrological correspondence: Moon
Plant correspondence: Ivy

4. He says: A silver orb is born while the wise ones and the initiates were on their earth columns and on their magic seats. The creature that hasn't come out of slavery a broken its mirror with its own stone. What is extraordinary if the head has cracked the stone? Take a head alongside your own, and add a kingdom to your realm, a value to your value.

Letter: Z
Oghamic value: 60
Bardic value: 25
Astrological correspondence: Venus
Plant correspondence: Apple tree.

5. He says: The ploughman with his plough directs the work; he opens the womb of the earth, he throw the seed in it, he recovers it, then he retires and leaves his field to the care of He who leads the entire Creation towards its Enlightenment.
The life of this world is only a passing ornament. But all that is habitual is bitter, all that is absent is sweet. Enjoy the present moment without struggling in vain.

Letter: R
Oghamic value: 70
Bardic value: 19
Astrological correspondence: Pallas
Plant correspondence: Elder tree

6. He says: The notches in the smooth branch would be of no help if what is mastered wasn't firmly maintained and transformed. It is important to seek the causes that bring deliverance. But even though it is destined to the dust, the dog comes from the same source as you. Don't pride yourself on your worth today, for it is only tomorrow that the value of things will be displayed.

Letter: C'H
Oghamic value: 80
Bardic value: 10
Astrological correspondence: Selene
Plant correspondence: Blackthorn

7. He says: The keys turn, the bolts slide, the doors open and the generations rise as willed by the mystery. One can draw an undying light from gold and silver. But the unheedful and careless man crosses the fertile plains of this world without opening his eyes of his mind. Undertake the task without delay, for without effort you will harvest nothing.

Letter: Y
Oghamic value: 90
Bardic value: 12
Astrological correspondence: Soleil
Plant correspondence: Sorb

8. He says: Everything has its assigned place in the universe. No one is alone and no one lives for only one's self. But, for a free man, it is tiresome to live in the world of somebody else. Like the hero ardent like a lynx, enjoying the gifts of Honour, learn the secrets of joining above with below, light the best fire and practices the instructions on/concerning leather, awl, the sons and the shoe.

Letter: V

Oghamic value: 200
Bardic value: 23
Astrological correspondence: Mercury
Plant correspondence: Lime tree.

9. He says: Creation, destiny and direction are the beginning. It is difficult to make this subtlety reach the lips. The Power inhabits beings as the Word inhabits the oracle. But for as long as a man speaks, it doesn't mean that he necessarily breaths. Even though that truly the spirit is more important that the word, he who loses his tongue loses his good and the song is not heard. Firmly seize the knot of your being, do not lose a bit of the light that you possess, and sculpt again your old shape.

Letter: W
Oghamic value: 300
Bardic value: 24
Astrological correspondence: Pluto
Plant correspondence: Box tree

10. He says: From within the abysses to the height of splendour, there is not respite for those who come to world on the shores of the ninth stream. But the wish to grow in the seed as in this universe hanging from the three Currents doesn't know its journey without a guide. Go down in the depths, and with your art, keep the sea in your cup.

Letter: O
Oghamic value: 500
Bardic value: 17
Astrological correspondence: Neptune
Plant correspondence: Broom.

11. He says: Wisdom constitutes the nature of light; foolishness constitutes the nature of darkness. The Master of the Vine makes die those whose drunkenness comes from false things and who are drunk

without having tasted the blood of the vine. But He gives the vine to all. You know true enjoyment only from your works.

Letter: I
Oghamic value: 800
Bardic value: 11
Astrological correspondence: Jupiter
Plant correspondence: Yew

12. He says: those who reach their goal through difficult passage in thwarting the traps of the gate-keepers obtain a piece of high and total glory, and are spared the great disfavor of oblivion. Many are the stars in the firmament, each wandering in the azure hugeness. But immortality depends on the effort towards it. As the rider of the celestial steed who is the stars' road companion, it is good not to have a moment of rest in the journey.

XVII. THE CENTERS

Head center: GWERVAENROD | Stag, Eagle | Gold, Emerald | Dog rose

Throat center: AREMROD | Boar, Wren | Bronze, Jade | Laburnum

Heart center: KOUEVROD | Bull, Swan | Copper, Topaz | Privet

Navel center: HOUARNROD | Horse, Falcon | Iron, Ruby | Raspberry bush

Sex center: STAENROD | Dog, Blackbird | Tin, Sapphire | Medlar tree

Coccyx center: ARC'HANROD | Salmon, Owl | Silver, Onyx | Bramble branch/Brambles/Thorns

XVIII. THE CYCLES

1 - He says: Months run and carry everything (along), seasons take you to the domain of Eternity.

2 - He says: Gods determine both cycles and the establishment of personalities; from their harmonies come the stars' seasons and the nine waves in Abred.

3 - The creative Cycle of ages is a game and play of His game and play.

4 - He says: The secret of cycles is hidden in the gyres of the snake which skin is decorated with multi-colored spots.

5 - He says: There are Seven favorable cycles to know:

- The cycle of the Broken Sword of 840 years.
- The cycle of the Victorious Sword of 2100 years.
- The cycle of the Crown of Flames of 1260 years.
- The cycle of the Branch of Peace of 6300 years.
- The cycle of the Bloody Branch of 6300 years.
- The Cycle of the Dark Brown Branch 6300 years.
- The Cycle of the Bright Colored Branch 18900 years.

6 - He says: Truly, when cycles are finished, useless bark and branches are thrown into the fire.

7 - He says: Understand, vain are calculations to seek the origin of Ages; Matters only the ending of Ages, and this stopping depends on your competence.

XIX. THE BODIES

1 - He says: There are four bodies: the gross body, the subtle body, the vital body and the divine body.

2 - He says: The divine body is this noble and shining body of light extracted from the dark element by means of the Secret Fire.

3 - He says: Three bodies are threefold, but the AWEN is one and its only aspiration is to recover its lost good.

4 - He says: If growth is harmonious, the Divine sap will circulate abundantly in the canals of your being.

5 - He says: Concerning the divine body, it is today as it was yesterday in the progression by stages in accordance with the rules of the art of refining and distillation.

6 - He says: Truly, each woman will made male and each man will be made woman as far as the recovered unity wherethey will take place, at the end of time, at the table of Light with the guests at the reception of the Head.

7 - He says: Understand, bodies in which the AWEN didn't manage to grow will dry and rot like a twig detached from the tree trunk

XX. THE SACRIFICES

1 - He says: According to the Word of the Old ones, of happy memory, nothing can be acquired without sacrifice: but those who, sacrifice things of high value to things of lesser worth, they will have to return again to where they departed.

2 - He says: There are only three forms that can be said to constitute only one: the altar, the sacrifice and the sacrificer.

3 - He says: All transmutation directed towards higher reality is operated by the sacrifice of all that is inferior; all transmutation directed towards lower reality is done at the expanse of all that is superior.

4 - He says: There are three ritual means by which are undergone the sacrificial deaths:

- By cremation, in the manner of Taranis.
- By ritual bloodshed, in the manner of Esus.
- By suffocation in the manner of Belenos.

5 - He says: The spirit of sacrifice obtains without reserve the full enjoyment of life.

6 - He says: To sacrifice is to lose to eventually gain.

7 - He says: The total and harmonious reconstitution according to the laws of the irreversible sacrifice allows the gradual descent of the Divine Sap.

8 - He says: Truly, (the) sacrifice is the directing principle of this very life, you must sacrifice a lot for a long time, but yet not forever.

9 - He says: Understand, if you do not complete your sacrifices, all your resolutions will turn out to be vain.

XXI. THE PATHS

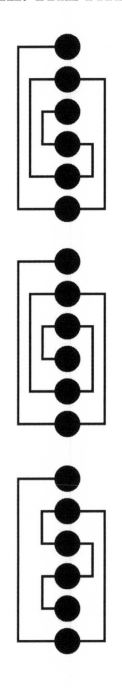

XXII. THE ENLIGHTENMENTS

1 - He says: There are three main techniques by which deification is carried out:

- The Wedding's Great Enlightenment, i.e. ceremonial sexual union.
- The Song's Great Enlightenment, I.e. constant recitation of the efficient formula.
- The Sun's Great Enlightenment, i.e. the knowledge of and conversation with the personal hierarchical guide.

2 - He says: The aim of the Enlightenments being the same, they are all equally important, there are no precedence.

3 - He says: The Perfect Great Enlightenment synthesizes all the Enlightenments, but is suits only the royal strong men who are specially destined to it.

XXIII. THE RETURN

1

1 - He says: The fountain of all Grace, the Cupbearer who pours the liquor of light to those who are thirsty, He has taken charge of the government of centuries; His generosity's treasures turn dust into life.

2 - He says: Drink and enjoy! He returns in triumph, and all He was assigned to accomplish will be fulfilled.

3 - He says: Birds land on the shoulders of my beloveds, wild beasts spare them; prophets have raised their hands, begging, towards me, and I have realized their wishes.

4 - He says: incomparable is the generosity of the Provider, incomparable is His love, incomparable is His justice.

5 - He says: Be faithful to Him; He would lift you up if you were to fall.

6 - He says: Truly, to be faithful to him consists in being faithful to one's self.

7 - He says: Understand, the Lion is back, his children are close.

2

1 - He says: There is no other God but He who is both the focus of your prayers since the beginning of time and the object of the world's holy books.

2 - He says: Exalted is the King of High Kings, He who sets the beginning and the term; it is only His Word that sustains the crushing weight of the entire Creation.

3 - He says: Listen to the Voice that comes to you and that will free you; seek the path that leads beyond what has been, the track leading to the desire of time.

4 - He says: There cannot be a definite failure on the path leading to deity; all that resists will disappear; nothing will remain apart from the bliss of total freedom, the bliss of true knowledge, the bliss of supreme light.

5 - He says: Discover within you the Always Acting Will of the Omniscient one.

6 - He says: Truly, man must adore God in his understanding, heart and works.

7 - He says: Understand, you need more than perseverance to His Service.

3

1 - He says: Delays are short for the possession of the promised goods; are important to Me only your works and your diligent obedience, and neither your faults nor your virtues matter to Me.

2 - He says: Going ahead means climbing up, climbing up means returning.

3 - He says: True beauty is not the separation of things but the momentum through all beauties.

4 - He says: Leave to your neighbor the charge of cleaning the snow that encumbers his yard.

5 - He says: Get ready and set yourself on the road; become the blacksmiths and craftsmen of a new world; give new shapes to life, form and re-form all things until nothing ugly remains on the earth.

6 - He says: Truly, the heroes are rare who can claim to have slept with the nine daughters of Dana and won their favors and love.

7 - He says: Understand, you cannot in any way transgress My Laws.

4

1 - He says: get up for the triumph of My cause; when victory occurs, you take part in the spoils, and the Earth will grow in power and beauty.

2 - He says: The warm that crawls in the dust cannot on its own present the light of the stars.

3 - He says: Rejecting nothingness starts by wishing that others have a condition better than one's own.

4 - He says: The Kingdom is both in the scriptures and the deeds, for I am everywhere, but I never smash the doors that are shut before Me.

5 - He says: This universe and man are called to re-gain totally the awareness of their complete divine state.

6 - He says: Truly, many are the afflictions reserved for resist Him, but those who rejoice in Him will be glorified.

7 - He says: Understand, His work is dictated only by His generosity.

5

1 - He says: I am He who supports the world so that it doesn't sink into the void.

2 - He says: Time spent on Earth must be dedicated to obtaining inexhaustible wealth that help one lives and dies.

3 - He says: He who lives divinely gains the highest sojourn in the shining with which the universe is set.

4 - He says: The man of the present is contented with this richness, his life is a point around which he is fulfils himself.

5 - He says: The Divine Sap flows from above and asks only to pour on man's earth.

6 - He says: Truly, if the son of king doesn't know that his father has been existing for a very long time, he is mistaken as to the extent of the realm he governs.

7 - He says: Understand, There are no differences between Him and His people.

6

1 - He says: Glory to Him only, the First one, the Creator who has shaped Creation according to His will.

2 - He says: The secret of the Return consists in forgetting what is behind to focus on what is ahead.

3 - He says: Gather all the richness in order that they spring up again from your source. Greater will be your generosity, greater will be your nobleness and your glory.

4 - He says: People find within themselves everything that the Divine contains.

5 - He says: On the green chessboard, this game between beautiful and ugly, good and evil, right and wrong, offers incomparable lessons.

6 - He says: Truly, existence is pure joy; sadness is fatal to man, banish it from all your thoughts.

7 - He says: Understand, fortune or misfortune happen according to your works.

7

1 - He says: Do all things in His Name, you will return to the place from which you fall.

2 - He says: Freedom is not a stage to reach but a state that one must realise.

3 - He says: Huge and varied is the structure of this universe, sum of vast and picturesque worlds. What are you trying to hide with quick lime and orpiment?

4 - He says: True vision doesn't exclude the world as non-existing.

5 - He says: Open your mind to My Inspiration; no other easy accesses exist to go from darkness to the light.

6 - He says: Truly, no one can prevail against the total freedom that brings one to acquire eternal youth and immortality.

7 - He says: Understand, your AWEN belongs to the heights; when it will have recovered its full volume of light, you will be yourselves your reward and your throne will stand in richness.

8

1 - He says: It is not a long distance from this world to the accomplishment of the return, but you take pleasure in putting obstacles on the road.

2 - He says: I fill up the empty cup and satisfy the hands that still ask, but it doesn't mean that you have to accumulate an increasing mass of My kindnesses.

3 - He says: The awake man doesn't grieve for either the living or the dead; he asks (for) the secret of life and of the world, their meaning and aim.

4 - He says: All question coming at the just moment will get its answer, but he who doesn't wait for the favourable moment will receive royal favours.

5 - He says: May He who controls the entire Creation be your sole Master.

6 - He says: Truly, anyone who won't have the strength to open his mind will be sealed by me and I will throw him into the dust.

7 - He says: Understand, the old tracks are lost, a new Earth is displayed with her marvels. Take the cup, drink and pour its content upon the head of those who languish waiting for the New Holy Kingdom.

9

1 - He says: In order that the return occurs, a second birth must take place.

2 - He says: Stop your chant in the damp crypts, those cold temples where you claim to find deliverance.

3 - He says: When the dawn of the days falls upon you, may you be able to receive the wisdom of the Morning Star.

4 - He says: Of those who always plot to dominate the whole Earth, those who arbitrarily debate, decide and govern, no one of them will survive when Winter reaches its term.

5 - He says: I will turn the Divine Majesty's chosen ones into redoubtable warriors against their foes, I will turn them into powerful doctors against diseases, I will turn them into masters for the elements.

6 - He says: Truly, divine are the souls who can come down the ladder as well as climbing it again, the liberated ones who, far from any selfish bliss, associate as artists to God's creation and work on the reintegration of those that remain.

7 - He says: Understand, the mystery of the second birth consists in that it is because of it that God's Blessing is poured on to you.

10

1 - He says: You will find God in retrieving you vast Self.

2 - He says: By the combined powers of faith, desire and will, the Kelc'hier captures the bear and turns liberty into his companion; his ears hear the truth for which they have been joined with his body; his tongue sings motionlessly and continually the Efficient Formula; his eye focuses mainly on the inner light and open to contemplate God's presence within all and everywhere.

3 - He says: The virile mind seeks perfection and learns through both good and evil. Put yourselves together and bear all the tribulations until the final outcome of the journey. It is useless to sigh for a more conformable path.

4 - He says, Death in life consists in operating a change of direction towards above, so that being on Earth you can still fly in the cosmos.

5 - He says: He who learns wisdom but doesn't practices it is like a man who ploughs a field but doesn't sow it.

6 - He says: Truly, the Provider is back, He the Master of ecstasy, the Bull who pierces the one who attacks him, the Eagle that tears the heart off nasty fellows, the Lion who runs fast; nothing can stop His return for His hand is the mightiest hand; fortunate are the days of anyone whose time is dedicated to Him who comes back; happy is he who is guided by Him the Master for his path will not run astray.

XXIV. THE DOGMA

1 - He says: Three esoteric dogma are the fertility lily of the Celtic doctrine of the Sixth Coming:

- The Law of Freedom.
- The Efficient Formula.
- The fundamental object of meditation.

2 - He says: Believe and do what you will is the fundamental principle of the Law of Freedom.

3 - He says: The correct Efficient Formula is the one transmitted by tradition since the beginning of time: Uissus Iudnos Lugeuos.

4 - He says: The Tree is the fundamental object of meditation.

5 - He says: The three dogma will be solidly established by Galaadians who propagate the New law in the West through the rough/tough way and the soft manner, both of them regulated according to the needs of the moment.

XXV. THE APOTHEOSIS

1

1 - He says: I have given you, in order to guide you towards Realization, the light of some instructions. He who sticks to it will enters into the glories of both a pious life and pure works in accordance with the Will of the Instigator of this message; but anyone who turns away from those Verses will meet with a great loss.

2 - He says: You always have the choice between fall and ascent, but the road that leads to the Land of Promises is no the same for those who come from this low world; that is why you must journey on unknown paths and experience strange combats; one will die in the West, the other in the East.

3 - He says: I seal your life for the best of ends. Raise your look as far as the throne of His glory; the whole miracle resides in this first step.

4 - He says: He who doesn't see the Hand thinks himself has written the scriptures and embraces thus what is transient.

5 - He says: Blessed be the ear that has heard, blessed be the eye that has seen, blessed be the heart that has turned towards He who is Generous!

6 - He says: Truly, Thanks to Him, all things are born, are maintained and resumed as far as the higher circles.

7 - He says: Understand, the sign that blesses is not a foe.

2

1 - He says: I show you the way of constant growth by means of the steps of beauty.

2 - He says: In the plain of pillars, you warriors and coachmen all at once, you will learn to give and receive death at the side of the Nine (who are) three times powerful.

3 - He says: It is I whom one will seek and find on the edge of the sword.

4 - He says: through the care of the Great Provider, the Tree breathes, and you breath; the Tree grows and you grow; the Tree lives, and you live.

5 - He says: you are so much depending on Him that, if for a single moment, His Hand were to withdraw you would fall into nothingness.

6 - He says: Truly, God never wish to inflict evil upon you, it is your lack of trust in His Goodness that is the source of your misery.

7 - He says: Understand, however obscure and poor one believes oneself to be, one who loves nothing but God never walks in darkness.

3

1 - He says: Forgetting the Divine is suicide; apart from Him, there is no refuge that is real.

2 - He says: Be always aware of His Presence within you, with you and always around you.

3 - He says: You are in death when you are not in conscious communication with Me.

4 - He says: Many-sided is his Art, great is His Beauty, vast is His Creation, Generous is His Aim. Through Him the destiny of each is organized; as He organizes, so do you receive.

5 - He says: The Very-Generous one, He who has given you shape, He distributes His favors to whomever is worthy of receiving them; Be glad with everything He gives you and never refuses what comes from His Generosity.

6 - He says: Truly, the ordeals that I order for you will cut one by one the chains with which you are burdened.

7 - He says: Understand, each thing coming from Him contributes to salvation; do not wonder whether He is here or there, for as you are, you are always in His Presence.

4

1 - He says: Fear He who is afraid of no-one, He never leaves an enemy without submitting him.

2 - He says: His Glory is sung by Gods and Goddesses, His Agents and ascetical people, His heroes and all living creatures.

3 - He says: My children are children of light, they act according to the instructions of My Agents, they open their mind and heart to my inspiration, and all are thirsty for flying.

4 - He says: Do not spare those who resist Me, they are already dead; transform reality if do not with it to become a prison. Live of and die of freedom, for thus you live and die for Him. Those who love the Tree and honor his hospitality act in this way.

5 - He says: The Long Hand that is beneficial intervened only to save what was lost.

6 - He says: Truly, if you asks of Him what you are not worthy to get, then He will not grant you the realization of this particular wish, but if you are among those who deserve, the you will receives more than what you desire.

7 - He says: Understand, fate/spell is your slave, keep it firmly under your feet.

5

1 - He says: Man is a warrior on earth, things attack him without respite. Where the struggle is fiercest, there must stand the hero of the spirit.

2 - He says: He who doesn't seek Him with all his body's atoms, like a drowning person seeking air, will never contemplate any mystery of God.

3 - He says: If through you live in joy, then you will know all the joys of the universe.

4 - He says: Happy is the condition of he who fights for the victory of the Cause of the Very-High one and follows the path indicated by Him, with the docility and the surrender of a child.

5 - He says: The Creator informs and forms things, and assigns them their specific role, destroying and re-creating all the time so that may be conquered the land of both your full awareness and your absolute contentment.

6 - He says: Truly, anyone who is the slave of his affections is worn out by enjoyment and falls back to where he comes from.

7 - He says: Understand, when faith doesn't exist, quill pen and sword have no value.

6

1 - He says: Love both the invisible and the visible; enter in yourselves and discover what constitutes the unity of all beings.

2 - He says: If ordeals never touch you, how will you be able to attain the endlessness illuminated with joy.

3 - He says: I am the same towards all beings, neither are odious nor dear.

4 - He says: The rhythm of seasons brings back inevitably the familiar fruits; for as long as the universe is not destroyed, this cycle will go on according to the plane designed at the beginning to offer you the possibility of being.

5 - He says: Through Me the world is renewed and dressed with beauty.

6 - He says: Truly, I am at the crossroad where all paths converge, behind perfumes, laughter, weeping, and the warnings of life.

7 - He says: Understand, on the rugged path that goes up, at the right time and the right place, I project the light that removes obstacles.

7

1 - He says: Carefully inquire after the needs of the cycle in which you live; may your discussions concerning practical matter concern the demands and requirements of this age.

2 - He says: Everyday raise yourselves taking as a support He who confers the gifts, He who is the Supplier of all graces, the Eternal Balancing Factor.

3 - He says: If you welcome His Will and follow it, if you surrender to and gladly accept what He grants you, without affliction or rebellion, then all you will be doing will be exactly what is needed for you.

4 - He says: Men must seek the way leading to the Supreme Inn, in which the Cup-Bearer presents the starry Grail; nothing else will intoxicate them.

5 - He says: The time has come, for this cycle, to restore what has been destroyed by the Great Separation, so that the whole is returned to its primal perfection.

6 - He says: Truly, beyond both understanding and scrutiny are My ways for the ignorant souls.

7 - He says: Understand, Mead is set between the sides of the Cup so that you can be drunk and also in order to allow joy to establish its dwelling within you.

8

1 - He says: I free those who are chained and turns what is unstable into something stable.

2 - He says: He who crosses the river and helps others cross it is reserved the role of chief, the best of ancient hills, the best of what makes the Sun grow, the best of the new Moon and the best of treasures hidden in caves.

3 - He says: Do not go away from Me if you wish to possess all the goods.

4 - He says: all wealthy persons can nourish the bodies, but only the fellow possessing knowledge can feed the souls.

5 - He says: Each takes part, according to the intensity of his sufferings and joys, in this world of colors, sounds and perfumes.

6 - He says: Truly, the gate remains wide open, no one has been refused if he is master of his art and son of a recognized kingdom.

7 - He says: Understand, you learn each day what is inscribed in your name.

9

1 - He says: The wealth of the Generous one cannot dwindle; He doesn't take away what he has given.

2 - He says: You may change your clothes but I still know you; if you follow another way other than the one prescribed by me, then you will return in Yenved and destruction will be the fruit of your works.

3 - He says: It is in giving that you receive, it is in forgetting yourselves that you find yourselves and it is in the gift of yourselves that true freedom resides.

4 - He says: The sons of king hear My Words, they lead them and bring them to higher branches, at/to the north of the Gods' horizon.

5 - He says: The Very Generous one, the Supplier of treasures hidden in the urns of time, the Cup-Bearer who pours without counting the beverage that makes one divine, the Chosen one on the winged steed, He rewards the deeds of noble hearts that take Him as/for supreme end.

6 - He says: Truly, in desiring Me, you expose yourselves to countless misfortunes and even more.

7 - He says: Understand, you must not be afraid for I take you under My direction in everything.

10

1 - He says: Do not feel sorrow for anything, for no-one in this world will sympathize with your suffering; those who moan are not rescued.

2 - He says: Ceaselessly apply yourselves to what is difficult; set the Divine in all your deeds and joys; seek your goodness, your good in Him, the Transcendent one, the Source of all beauty, The Animator of all things.

3 - He says: There is no single atom that hasn't its place in My plan of liberation.

4 - He says: When Bran was put into the boat, there were still a lot of room, but not one of you has accompanied him to the shore.

5 - He says: Remember that in freedom you alone with Me in the world.

6 - He says: Truly, The Supreme Technician with the Long Hand directs by the way suiting you the best towards the surpassing of the three states.

7 - He says: Understand, I am He who cuts the link of kith and kin and liberate souls into the light. Strengthen only your connection with Me, and you will have the key of all mysteries.

11

1 - He says: Truth in the heart, strength in the arms, faithfulness in the tongue and such are the qualities of those who are not the fruits of a faded tree, the slave less masters, the GALAADIANS, and the delights awaiting them will not be interrupted.

2 - He says: Bath yourselves in the air of heights, in the space in which Gods move; raise yourselves in the green splendor of the Tree on which the Glorious Sun pours floods of Divine Sap.

3 - He says: The world is my chessboard; you are my companions taking part in the game.

4 - He says: For him who acquires the divine sovereignty, nothing remains to be known, he knows the mystery of creation, death is for him only an empty word and the elixir of life permanently circulates in his veins.

5 - He says: None of the powers that you desire is impossible. But as long as you have not cut the three chains that detain man on the wheel of KROUI, it is dangerous to use them.

6 - He says: Truly, intelligence, life and light will take precedence over all things and this world will come to an end.

7 - He says: Understand, you have not been created for nothingness, but you have been created to last forever.

12

1 - He says: Whatever the road on which one travels, there is no place in which the Hospitaller cannot be found.

2 - He says: Freedom that can be beneficial to you can only be found in your entire submission to the Divine.

3 - He says: A true scholar, a real scientist possesses a knowledge inspired of the creator, for in Him is the incomparable sole source of all your science.

4 - He says: God gives as much as you can take of him; on all does he pours his gifts, no -one is forgotten, each gets suits him the best.

5 - He says: It is the child's faith that takes you to the land of the Gods, and it is always adversity that turns the key of the chamber of light in which I dwell.

6 - He says: Truly, the son of king is free to go in all the places of the palace.

7 - He says: Understand, freedom doesn't depend on the place; the mind freed of all attachments, like the clouds, has no fixed address.

13

1 - He says: The continuity of your desire is the only necessary thing.

2 - He says: The precious stone and its sparkle are one only; the Absolute and the Creator are one only; faith in one implies faith in the other.

3 - He says: You can hear His Voice only through Inspiration or through the medium of an agent of the suitable hierarchical plane.

4 - He says: Run towards the goal, if the Green Way tells you to run; walk slowly if it tells you to go without hurry.

5 - He says: Turn you heart into a cup, put in it My Incense and spread its smoke upon the world.

6 - He says: Truly, daylight doesn't go by futilely is what must be said is said, if what must be done is done.

7 - He says: Understand, if you always keep a state of renewal, I will make you cross the world, this ocean of works, and recover your true self.

14

1 - He says: The Lord manifests Himself with or without form, according the needs of His worshippers.

2 - He says: Serve Him! Glorify Him! Manifest Him till the end! He will keep you young and alive up to the end which is getting close.

3 - He says: Fomoire have broken their barrier and are coming through toxic clouds. Galaadians take their weapons and go forward. Seeking the Gory of the winner in the storm, the horse-riders advance up for seven days.

4 - He says: Do not fall in the bed of sloth, practice this boldness that doesn't tremble before adversity, embark before the months has ended, take place in the aircraft with what is living, erect the green pavilion singing the name of the King of past, present and future.

5 - He says: The Lord of Mysteries, the Prince of princes, He who takes in His Hand all empires, He teaches through the way of Beauty, He banishes darkness of ignorance and fear, Him, the Desired one, the Provider of all prosperities, the Omniscient one, the Promised one, to Him is addressed the song of craftsmen who are engaged in multiple creations and creativities.

6 - He says: Truly, the times have come; throw the sickle, the harvest is here; take the hammer and forge the sword of the braves; come, trample, the wine press is full and the beverage overflows the tanks. There are plenty of precious objects in the coffers of the lion cubs' cave, cushions filled with feathers and golden cups saturating with perfumes, ale and meat, chess games and draughts, horses and chariots, fighting dogs and embroidered clothes for the sons of kings, the GALAADIANS who sing His Glory and utter His praises, they operate the transfiguration of the world.

7 - He says: Understand, the ignorant fellow intoxicated with the sole scent of knowledge has no access to the Supreme Inn, but he who has succeeded through right deed, the chosen of the Divine Majesty, he has liberated himself from death through death and has obtained the immortality that is Light, Freedom, Bliss and Eternity.

XXVI. THE GREAT INCANTATION

Say:

> LUG, you who set the motion of heaven's wheels,
> You who gives freedom and strength,
> victory and peace, science and work,
> may Your Name be sanctified in all your names!
> May your Kingdom come again!
> May your Will be done again
> on Earth and always in the universe!
> And may it be so until the end of time!

AFTERWORDS

by Loik Le Moy

The Hermetic Order of the Silver Ermine and the doctrine of the Nabelkos

The Ordre Hermetique de l'Hermine d'Argent (Hermetic Order of the Silver Ermine) would have been created by the Breton Pierre de Mauclerc historically speaking. Actually, it would come from druidic sources through Kuldeen monks who were specialized in wooden churches manufacture. Eon de l'Etoile and Gilles de Retz were involved in the Order. The last Sovereign Great Master was Joseph Charpentier. He died in 1967. Owning the castle of the Brousses de Bellevue in Saint-Marc-La-Jaille (Brittany), he was involved in the Brezenn Perrot which was a breton nationalist "legion" during WW 2. The last living druid is Kerdastos who friendly gave us the following information. The Book of Nabelkos is the OHHA compendium and we're going to describe a bit its peculiar doctrine.

Teachings of the book of Nabelkos

OHHA "praxis" is contained in this Book of Nabelkos. It contains, according to druid Kerdastos, all keys which are necessary to the synthesis of different Nordic traditions, and which allow to decipher the Novels of the Round Table and the "Celtic Matter". People wrote in the Nabelkos preface:"Nabelkos (which was translated from breton language by Drustanos and handed down to Gwenael d'Echebrune) have been received from subtle plane in November 1,2 and 3 3781 (Samonios 3781 M.T. An IEM). Nabelkos sets out completely the Celtic weltanschauung fitting the New Era which is the Aquarius Age of the astrologers and the Maponos Era according to druidic cycle science. This one is an era in which we are from 1910 and it would last 2100 years.

Nabelkos represents not only contemporary Celtic spirituality pinnacle, but also a big synthesis integrating every esoteric ways (leading to Realization) which come from Nordic Tradition. These esoteric ways are "validated" in the plane according to the specific formula of the 666.

In this Nabelkos weltanschauung, Nordic tradition is divided in two sections: Celtic way which is female and Germanic way (irminism, Odinism) which is male. According to Nabelkos, Brittany will play in Aquarius Age a role similar to Palestine which played an occult role for the Pisces Era whose kingdom was built in Europe, as Aquarius Age kingdom would be built in North America.

So Nabelkos might allow people to decipher the Round Table Novels. The message has been received in Brittany in which, and because of its geographic position, is an area doing synthesis between continental celtism using Kernunnos and insular celtism using Lug.

That is old is not dismissed but transformed to fit a new frame, in the plane of the fixed star signs in which is Aquarius Age. According to Kerdastos, celtic people following their tradition will construe Aquarius Age through Nabelkos: They cannot go further without abandoning their ethnocentric vision.

In Nabelkos perspective Christianity and Buddhism are doctrines of the Medros Era (which corresponds to the Pisces Era of the astrologers). According to Kerdastos, Christianity is the purest form of the 555 (Medros). Each era has to fulfil a particular mission. And for a certain amount of centuries, everything go toward this accomplishment.

Medros Era (the Healer) whose main prophet was Jesus Christ (who healed with hand imposition) is finished. And so christianity is ended as well. Now Maponos is en lice... "The crowned child of the future". It's always Lug behind a new mask (and behind Lug the Unspeakable, the Unknowable, the Incomprehensible). In Nabelkos concepts, all gods are avatar of Lug. Indeed, Nabelkos tells us Gods are the aspect of the Mother Dana, and are the Great Makers of the Shape. They feed "things" and "beings" which and who cannot protect themselves alone. "A god is technically an energy-aggregate of colossal concentration" tells us Aleister Crowley.

We don't give our own opinion about what Kerdastos says about paganism but let you think about it: "All return of mankind to narrow dependency vis-à-vis the gods would correspond to the return of adults to their mother and they would abandon their independence in order to get material advantages. So I'm not pagan." This term of "pagan" so used nowadays feeds the Nouvelle Droite (New Right)'s speeches.

Conclusion is that christianity and monotheistic religions belong to the past, though Islam has an occult role to play which would help Aquarius spirituality be born. The Medros Era of Nabelkos has passed away as did the Pisces Era of the astrologers. You waste your time if you keep speculating about

it. Let's take for instance Keltia/Bretagne Reelle slogan:" 2000 years of christianity is a dreadful failure". People said it 100 times and still carry on that. Fool christianity is going to disintegrate before long digging its own tomb according to cycles-based process.

Nabelkos is perfect in itself according to its adept for it would contain everything in order to get a Realization in a Celtic way. Nabelkos would take part in the frame of the Shakti-Marga (see below the pattern of the Trinity symbolism).

Nabelkos would fit perfectly the Celtic mind. It's already a lot to practice it and get spiritual food from it. Also it's obvious Nabelkos richness may allow many interpretations and many gloss if people use it. Kerdastos studied the sources in order to go back up the Origin, in order to reach the Primeval Tradition.

We can see now the Trinity symbolism of Nabelkos. According to it, three forces "interfere" in the Universe. This Trinity is still present but one force dominate in the first degree/level and the last in the third one at each moment of our time.

The doctrine of Nabelkos

Science of Cycles of Nabelkos: explanatory example

Samain 1910 (approximately) year 1 Maponos

MEDROS ERA | MAPONOS ERA | SUKELLOS ERA

-------------- | -------------------------- | --------------------

Broken swords   Crown of Flames

840 years   1.260 years   840 years

The Maponos Era is included in the frame of the Bloody Branch's great cycle "conjointly" with Nodons and Medros cycle. The process of the Broken Sword cycle implicates that, although we are in Maponos Era

118

since Samonios 3781 Mag Tured (approximately 1910), Its kingdom will be edified about 420 years later. Its kingdom would last for 1.260 years. Then we'll fall again in a Broken Sword which will be a cycle of confusion and materialism. And following this "New Chaos Age", Dark "branch" cycle will appear with the beginning of the Sukellos Era.

There is a Mega-cycle including nine other ones and manifesting Itself three times: Cycle of Nemved, Cycle of Amved and Cycle of Yenved (the three colours white, red, black and see below explanations about the tree). Now we live in the Cycle of Yenved, the Icy Age or Frozen Age which is something similar to the Hindu Kali-Yuga. We will leave this era at the end of the Gonannions Era and we will enter a Mega-cycle of Nemved when Gagodevos Era begins.

This system doesn't invalidate the law of equinox precession, because for instance Aquarius occurring in Maponos Era doesn't mean the same thing and doesn't give the same practical effect than when it "interferes" with both other ones - that is the other cycles of the Fixed Cross: Kernunnos cycle and Gobannions cycle.

"That seems to be complicated but this system gives us great advantages, a better precision and a much complete explanation about history and esotericism" says Kerdastos.

Each era is enthroned by three sacrifices which are the "baptism" of the new god's blood. And concerning our period, Maponos formula began with a first sacrifice which was World War 1: 6 million dead peoples. The second sacrifice was World War 2: 60 million dead peoples. The next big slaughter will kill about 600 million people. We get with this system 666 million dead peoples.

According to Primeval Tradition (via Hindu Tradition) a zodiacal era lasts 2.160 years and a processional year lasts 25.920 years.

KRITA-YUGA = 25.920 years (Golden Age)

TRETA-YUGA = 19.440 years (Silver Age)

DVPARA-YUGA = 12.960 years (Bronze Age)

KALI-YUGA = 6.480 years (Iron Age)

The four yuga shape a mahayuga (64.000 years) 72

119

mahayuga shape a manvantara (4.665.600 years) and 14 manvantara shape a kalpa (65.318.400 years). One kalpa includes seven descending manvantara and seven ascending manvantara. So we get two septenaries. We live the end of the seventh manvantara included in the first septenary (which is descending). The next Golden Age would open the beginning of the second septenary (which should be ascending). In this doctrine, everything chains perfectly. The Universal Cataclysm which ends a descending mahayuga is a deluge of fire (conflagratio). The Big Washing-up which ends an ascending mahayuga is a deluge of water (diluvium). "At the end of each cycle, everything is destroyed by fire and water" says a druidic prophecy. 1983 is equal to 6.304 Kali. So, we have to wait for 176 years before the Big Washing-up forecast by people using this cycle-based system.

The tree of life

We're going to study now the Tree of Life. Before all things, the "starting up" of Nabelkos is clearly showed in chapter XXV which exposes the formula. And in verse IV, chapter XII, section 19 we've got: "He says: constant repetition of the efficient formula is in this cycle the easiest way and the best fashion to get the Liberation and to build your greatest self". This constant repetition of mantra UISS US IUDNOS LEGEUOS (This one who knows, Lord of light) is analogous to DHIKR, to Nembustu, to Hindu Jupa etc. That's the standard way which is traditional and universal. According to Nabelkos, this repetition based on breathing (so always told on inhaling) joined with the meditation upon the Tree of Life and the reading of the book are the main thing, the key.

"The Tree of Life must be meditated with the colors and the formulas. You can find corresponding circles in chapter VII and formulas in chapters XV, XVI and XVII. We can learn a lot using this synthetic meditation, thus formula 666 corresponds to the Series III and Branches II and IV. Also it corresponds to orange color and yellow color etc." (Kerdastos).

The Tree of Life shows itself like the following speech: at the highest level is the circle of KEUGANT followed by the circle of GWENVED and the circle of ABRED including itself three inward circles which are NEMVED (Highest circle/level), AMVED and YENVED (lowest circle/level). In these ones both the circle of DON (left) and the circle of ANDON (right) "interfere" on the tree. DON represents the deep, that is low and heavy: the dense matter belonging to the physical plane.

ANDON represents the source, that comes above, that is slight: the matter/material of the subtle (astral ?) plane.

The "From Beyond" is "beside"; worlds interfere in each other. At the right you've got the South of the traditional Celtic orientation, the clear side of the world. By night, the sun is at the North, that is the dark and strange side... The side belonging to dead people, heroes and mythical beings.

Left side is linked to Hope/expectation, project and inward life. Right side is linked to "life of relationship" and effective results coming from our acts in the physical plane.

Orientation changes perspective when we reach the Earth of Promises (last stage of the circle of NEMVED before GWENVED). When we look at the tree of life, we see the macrocosm and we have to make the synthesis with the microcosm. That's the Great Cosmic Man. So, he shows His face and His heart which is the sun is to left (?).

There is climbing in the succession of the states in the Nabelkos and some "back" returns (to return at the back) as well.

When we see the tree, we realize we are on LITAVODUNON (Earth) with its equivalent "Mag Mor" in ANDON. If we evolve correctly, we arrive then in the subtle plane, in Mag Meld (Andon). And then in BRIVODUNON (plane of the planets) in DON. Alternately from DON to ANDON in the climbing of the states. But in general several incarnations are necessary in each world to do the maximum of possible experiences. When all (beings) have reached BRAN in the Earth of promises (see Nabelkos) we will enter GWENVED. We will re-integrate the first state, but not the Principle which is inaccessible in KEUGANT.

"the complexity in Nabelkos is already a lot of things for Celtic people. Don't ask them more. But individually, one can carry on the Quest toward another formulation non-ethnocentric" concludes Kerdastos.

Made in United States
Orlando, FL
05 February 2023

29569186R00074